DIRECT INSTRUCTION

The Instructional Design Library

Volume 22

DIRECT INSTRUCTION

Siegfried Engelmann
University of Oregon
Oregon Research Institute
Eugene, Oregon

Danny G. Langdon
Series Editor

Educational Technology Publications
Englewood Cliffs, New Jersey 07632

Library of Congress Cataloging in Publication Data

Engelmann, Siegfried.
    Direct instruction.

    (The Instructional design library; v. 22)
    Bibliography: p.
    1. Reading (Primary) 2. Education, Primary.
3. Education--Experimental methods. I. Title.
II. Series: Instructional design library; v. 22.
LB1525.E58   372.4'1   79-24814
ISBN 0-87778-142-7

Copyright © 1980 Educational Technology Publications, Inc., Englewood Cliffs, New Jersey 07632.

All rights reserved. No part of this book may be reproduced or transmitted, in any form or by any means, electronic or mechanical, including photocopying, recording, or by any information storage and retrieval system, without permission in writing from the Publisher.

Printed in the United States of America.

Library of Congress Catalog Card Number: 79-24814.

International Standard Book Number: 0-87778-142-7.

First Printing: March, 1980.

FOREWORD

Direct Instruction is one of the most highly structured and programmed instructional designs that I have reviewed. It leaves nothing to chance during implementation. Those who see tight structure in learning on the negative side will find this design distasteful. However, there are many students who have difficulty in learning with traditional methods. Perhaps the structure suggested in this book may be the solution for these students.

One of the impressive things about this book is the obvious attention the author has given to grounding the design in learning theory (or, from his viewpoint, learning practice). The author has done his homework! He suggests many worthwhile considerations for almost any instructional design. I, for one, will try his ideas in my own instructional efforts.

Danny G. Langdon
Series Editor

PREFACE

I thank the people who helped me piece together this work, particularly Sarah Norris and Susan Brewster, for attending to the countless details that eluded me. To them, three kisses each and four pounds of thanks.

Also a few pounds of gratitude to Danny G. Langdon. I told him that I would finish the manuscript by a particular date, that I am super-compulsive, and that he could rely on me to get it done in time. I then proceeded to be quite late, and he graciously did not remind me about my earlier chest-beating.

Finally, Doug Carnine deserves special cheers. Over the past years, he has taken nearly every assertion that the Direct Instruction approach makes about analyzing concepts of teaching and has designed very carefully controlled experiments that test these assertions—over 50 of them. Although much of his research is gathering dust in unpublished technical reports, Doug's work has helped us gain a more precise understanding of some research problems and of communicating with others in the field of instructional design.

S.E.

CONTENTS

FOREWORD v

PREFACE vii

ABSTRACT xi

   I. USE 3

   II. OPERATIONAL DESCRIPTION 13

   III. DESIGN FORMAT 37

   IV. OUTCOMES 79

   V. DEVELOPMENTAL GUIDE 85

   VI. RESOURCES 97

VII. APPENDIX 105

ABSTRACT

DIRECT INSTRUCTION

The Direct Instruction approach begins with the question, "What is the most efficient way to teach each skill?" not with the question, "How do children typically learn each skill?"

The learner is assumed to act in a perfectly reasonable way, which means that the learner will always derive an interpretation that is consistent with the presentation the learner receives. If the presentation of examples is consistent with more than one interpretation, the learner will derive one of these interpretations—not necessarily the one the teacher wishes. Conversely, the presentation that is consistent with only one interpretation will work with virtually all learners who have necessary preskills.

The Direct Instruction approach classifies discriminations as choice-response discriminations (that call for yes-no or binary responses), production-response discriminations (requiring the learner to name or produce examples), and sentence-relationship discriminations. Any discrimination of a given type can be taught through a variation of the same sequence. For instance, any choice-response discrimination can be processed through a variation of the same sequence, and it will teach because it will convey only one interpretation.

Since variations of the same model sequence will work for all discriminations of a given type, diagnostic teaching is possible to identify the type of discrimination called for by a task, designing a sequence to teach the discrimination.

Complex routines for solving problems are constructed so the same routine works for all problems of a given type. The steps that lead to the outcome are made functional and overt. The teacher now has the opportunity to provide precise feedback.

In addition to dealing with teaching discriminations and complex routines, Direct Instruction is concerned both with the expansion and application of skills that are taught as well as with the teaching of new motor behaviors. The same goal applies to all skills—teach them in the most efficient manner possible.

DIRECT INSTRUCTION

I.
USE

General

Direct Instruction is an approach to establishing new behavior and maintaining it. Because of its broad orientation, Direct Instruction applies to nearly all instructional problems, from the teaching of very unfamiliar behaviors to a handicapped youngster to turning on older students who are not easy to motivate. It applies to the teaching of college level skills and to the teaching of subjects not taught well through traditional approaches—reading, spelling, arithmetic, and the sciences.

Although Direct Instruction has potential application to a nearly unlimited range of instructional situations, it has been used primarily in "hard-to-teach" situations. The reason is that these situations provide a better demonstration of the approach's effectiveness because these are situations in which teachers typically feel most frustrated and in need of help. If a Direct Instruction application works with higher performing, easy-to-teach children, the teachers' response may be: "Yes, the results are somewhat better than those of other approaches we have used, but are these extra benefits worth the additional amount of work required by using this approach? After all, the other approaches we have used also work." In the hard-to-teach situation, other approaches typically have *not* worked. The additional preparation and training required by the Direct Instruction approach are therefore more readily justified. The comparison is not between two approaches that work but between one that doesn't and one that permits the teacher to reach the instructional objective.

As several statements above imply, Direct Instruction requires more work than most other approaches. It requires a careful analysis of the skill that is to be taught, a careful analysis of the learner, and very careful execution of the presentation that is designed to "teach" or to establish the new behavior. We will see that Direct Instruction teaching controls every controllable variable that affects the learner's performance. For the teacher of a young, naive learner, this control means "acting" out a prescribed sequence that is all but choreographed. The use of the hands, the timing of the words, the responses to the learner, the signaling for the learner to respond—all are controlled. For the designer of Direct Instruction, control means constructing a presentation that ideally works across an enormous range of individual student variation.

An ideal presentation is created when the instructional variables (the examples, the wording, the tasks) are adequately controlled and when the teacher's behavior in executing the presentation (the pacing, inflection, corrections) is controlled. The ideal, of course, is not always achievable. For the teacher, the goal of being an impeccable Direct Instruction presenter is analogous to becoming a proficient dancer, gymnast, or pianist. Great amounts of practice and work are needed. Without sufficient training and feedback, the teacher will probably not attain the ideal. The teacher may be successful at working with average performers but will probably lack the skill needed to communicate through examples with lower performers.

Just as the teaching presentation may fall short of the ideal, the design of the presentation may be less than ideal. Tasks may be too difficult; the presentation may not provide enough practice on particular responses; and the concept or skill being taught may not articulate as well as it should with related discriminations the learner is being taught.

Although practical problems exist and although achieving the ideal communication between teacher and learner is not always possible, the idea behind Direct Instruction is to control every possible detail that makes a difference in how the ideas will be communicated to the learner—to make the material interesting but above all to make it sound.

Commercial instructional programs based on Direct Instruction principles include the following programs published by Science Research Associates (SRA):
- *DISTAR Reading* (levels 1, 2, and 3)
- *DISTAR Arithmetic* (levels 1, 2, and 3)
- *DISTAR Language* (levels 1, 2, and 3)
- *Corrective Reading* programs:
    - Decoding levels A, B, and C
    - Comprehension levels A, B, and C

Other Direct Instruction programs are published by E-B Press. These include:
- *Programmed Time Telling*, Hofmeister, A., Atkinson, C.M., Hofmeister, J.B.
- *E-B Press Intermediate Math Series*, Steely, D.
- *The Morphographic Spelling Series*, Dixon, R.

Effectiveness

The largest body of data supporting the tenets of Direct Instruction is the comparison of Follow Through sponsors. The Follow Through comparison is probably the largest educational experiment that has been conducted, involving over 15,000 children in 60 communities. The program was set up so that selected school districts cooperated with program sponsors, each to implement a sponsor's approach. Each participating community had a choice of sponsors, ranging from those that promoted individualized instruction or cognitive development modeled after Piaget, to those advocating behavioral approaches. The goal of all sponsors was to provide successful instruction for disadvantaged children in grades K through three or one through three. The National evaluation was conducted in 1972 and 1973.

The instruments used to assess the children's performance included the Metropolitan Achievement Test, the Coopersmith Self-Esteem Inventory, and the Intellectual Achievement Responsibility Scale (used to measure self-image). Below is a brief description of the major sponsors:

1. *Responsive Education Model (Far West Laboratory for Educational R and D).* This model, based on the work of Glen Nimnicht, is highly "eclectic." Techniques include those used by O.K. Moore (the "Talking Typewriter"), Maria Montessori, and Martin Deutsch. "The learning environment... is made up of a number of learning centers; each center focuses on different concepts or tasks. The child's individual interest determines the child's choice of learning centers" (Nero and Associates, 1976, p. 91).

2. *Tucson Early Education Model (TEEM—University of Arizona).* Similar to the language-experience approach espoused by Sylvia Ashton Warner (1963), the TEEM program hinges on language development. TEEM, like the Responsive Education program, works from the child's interests. "Teaching elaborates on and explores what is already salient for the children—their environment and their current interests" (Maccoby and Zellner, 1970, pp. 15-16). The assumption is, "If language is made useful and if language and the written word surround the child, he will easily learn" (p. 16).

3. *Open Education (EDC)—Education Development Center.* "There is a rich environment of materials for children to explore. They are encouraged to initiate activities, be self-directing, and become intensely involved in their interests.... The time schedule is flexible, permitting children to learn according to their individual rhythms of engagement and disengagement" (Maccoby and Zellner, 1970, p. 6).

4. *Cognitively Oriented Curriculum—High/Score Educational Research Foundation.* David Weikart's Follow Through program elaborates on the Piagetian theme. "The focus is on the development of children's ability to reason" (Abt Associates, 1977, p. 211). The program "focuses on the underlying cognitive processes that enable the child to acquire and organize knowledge of the world. It provides for the challenging of emerging abilities, builds on the child's interests, talents, and long-term goals, and applies these emerging abilities to concepts and skills in a wide range of subject and activity areas" (Nero and Associates, 1976, p. 151).

5. *Florida Parent Education Model—University of Florida.* While not prescribing classroom curricula or organization, the sponsor provides parent educators who spend part of their time in the classroom and serve as the link between school and home. These educators instruct parents in the presentation of different activities. "The aim is to create tasks that are soundly based on Piagetian educational philosophy. Lessons are designed to give a child meaningful experiences with a balance between the cognitive, affective, and psychomotor skill areas of the child's life" (Nero and Associates, 1976, p. 279).

6. *Bank Street College Model—Bank Street College of Education.* Bank Street College of Education has long been an advocate of the early childhood education philosophy espoused by Headstart and middle-class, traditional nursery schools. The program is basically eclectic, incorporating strands of philosophy from Dewey, Piaget, and Freud.

7. *Behavior Analysis Model—University of Kansas.* The Behavior Analysis model "believes in a systematic and precise use of positive reinforcement" (Nero and Associates, 1976, p. 314). Its primary objective is not expressed in global or societal terms, but in the children's mastery of reading, arithmetic, handwriting, and spelling skills. Acquisition of

academic and social skills is reinforced with praise and tokens which can be traded for desired activities during "exchange" periods.

8. *Southwest Educational Development Laboratory (SEDL).* The primary focus of the SEDL program is language development. A bilingual approach is used where appropriate. The assumption is made that the child will demonstrate "an increased capacity to learn English and develop literacy in two languages if instruction is given in the native language" (Nero and Associates, 1976, p. 210). The reading program is based on a sequential presentation of oral subject matter followed by the same subject matter in written form. The programmed materials used by SEDL have been developed in both English and Spanish models.

9. *Direct Instruction Model—University of Oregon.* The Direct Instruction model "is based on the assumption that every child can achieve well in school if he or she receives adequate instruction; conversely, pupil failure is a direct result of instructional failure. Disadvantaged children lag behind in developing relevant skills, particularly language concepts used in the school. For classroom success in these skills, their learning rate must be accelerated to reach the achievement levels of non-disadvantaged children" (Nero and Associates, 1976, p. 348). The DISTAR programs are used in all Direct Instruction Follow Through sites. Maccoby and Zellner observe that "Engelmann and Becker reason that it is not necessary to make a special effort to raise the self-esteem of the children; they believe that high self-esteem will be a by-product of competence" (1970, p. 9).

The children in the Direct Instruction model outperformed children in all other models on total reading, total arithmetic, spelling, and language. Table 1 summarizes the data for Kindergarten-starting children who completed the third grade of the respective Follow Through programs. Note that the table is scaled in ¼ standard deviation units. (The difference

Table 1

*Comparison of Third-Grade Follow Through
Children on Academic Achievement Measures*

Language	Spelling	Total Math	Total Reading		Percentile
					11 16 23 31 40 50 60
50	51	48	41	Direct Instruction	L M S / R
18	19	15	15	Southwest Lab (SEDL)	R,M S L
20	32	14	24	Parent Education	M L R S
22	49	28	34	Behavior Analysis	L M R S
23	32	19	30	Bank Street	L M R S
18	28	17	28	Responsive Education	M L S,R
12	22	11	21	Cognitive Curriculum	M^L S R
22	27	18	26	TEEM (Arizona)	M L S R
19	18	14	18	Open Education (EDC)	M L S,R

between the 40th percentile and the 31st percentile, for example, is ¼ standard deviation.)

The differences in performance between sponsors are large, with those approaches that concentrate on individualization and psychodynamics typically performing low, while the approaches that stress control of environmental variables (Direct Instruction and Behavior Analysis) produce better results. The advantage of the Direct Instruction approach is most evident in total math (an advantage of 1/2 standard deviation above the next-highest sponsor), and language (an advantage of 3/4 standard deviation above the next-highest sponsor).

The comparison groups for the different Follow Through programs were not perfect matches with the Follow Through groups; therefore, the outcomes were statistically adjusted. After these adjustments, a comparison was made between each Follow Through sponsor and the comparison groups (Becker, 1977). If the adjusted difference between any Follow Through and the non-Follow Through comparison group showed a statistical significance in favor of the Follow Through program, the program received a plus. If the adjusted difference favored the comparison group, the Follow Through program received a minus. By counting the pluses for a given model, subtracting the minuses, and dividing by the number of comparisons, a ratio is achieved. If the ratio is positive, the overall effect of the sponsor may be judged positive.

Table 2 provides a summary of the major sponsors for basic skills, academic cognitive skills, and for affective outcomes.

Common criticisms of the Direct Instruction programs are that they promote rote learning and are not designed to teach cognitive skills. The outcomes of the Follow Through comparison suggest that this appraisal is unfounded. Although this Direct Instruction score for basic skills was the

Table 2

Relative Effects of Different Programs

	Basic Skills	Academic Cognitive Skills	Affective Outcomes
Direct Instruction	304.5	336.67	177.33
Southwest Lab (SEDL)	15.5	124.67	62.67
Parent Education	-10.5	-27.67	97.33
Behavior Analysis	-9.25	-115.33	128.33
Bank Street	-208.25	-69.33	-55.33
TEEM (Arizona)	-258.5	-266.67	-222.33
Responsive Education	-226.5	-122.67	-104.33
Open Education (EDC)	-312.5	-333.33	-166.67
Cognitive Curriculum	-361	-277.67	-222.33

highest of all sponsors (+304), the Direct Instruction approach achieved a cognitive outcome score of +337, while all but one of the other sponsors achieved negative scores. Similarly, the affective measure outcome for the Direct Instruction model (+177) was higher than that of any other sponsor.

Much of what you will read in the following chapters will run counter to your intuition. The emphasis of Direct Instruction on details may seem extreme. The analysis of the skills to be taught may strike you as pedantic. However, the approach *works,* even though it is less than uniformly endorsed by educators.

The remainder of this book will make occasional references to data; however, the main focus will not be on data but on the logic behind the approach, the specific principles that characterize the approach, and how you can use limited parts of the approach to meet specific teaching needs.

References

Abt Associates. *Education as Experimentation: A Planned Variation Model.* (Vol. II.) Boston: Author, 1977.

Becker, W.C. Teaching Reading and Language to the Disadvantaged. What We Have Learned from Field Research. *Harvard Education Review,* 1977, *47,* 518-543.

Maccoby, E.E., and Zellner, M. *Experiments in Primary Education.* New York: Harcourt, Brace, Jovanovich, Inc., 1970.

Nero and Associates. *The Follow Through Resource Guide.* Portland, Oregon: Nero and Associates, 1976.

Warner, S.A. *Teacher.* New York: Simon and Schuster, 1963.

II.

OPERATIONAL DESCRIPTION

To describe Direct Instruction, we will look at two teaching settings in which the teacher uses Direct Instruction. We will first look at the teaching of beginning reading, then at the teaching of equations skills to older students.

Communication Conventions

Although the two Direct Instruction presentations that we will sample differ in many ways, they share important features. These features stem from the need to communicate unambiguously with students.

1. The presentations are scripted, with specifications of exactly what the teacher is to say. The scripted presentation assures that the same wording is used for similar tasks. It also assures that the teacher uses clear, concise directions.

2. The teacher paces the presentation rapidly. It is a fact that faster paced presentations (more tasks per minute) result in better student attention and higher student performance. Slow presentations lead to wandering attention and more lapses in memory.

3. Many tasks are presented to the group, with all children responding in unison. The obvious advantage of this convention is that it provides for a greater number of responses for each child in the group. Instead of achieving a response from only one student, the teacher receives responses from all

students in the small group when a "group task" is presented. These tasks, therefore, are efficient.

4. To assure that all students "initiate" the responses called for by group tasks, the teacher uses signals to indicate precisely when a group response is to occur. Without signals, the teacher may discover that a few students in the group are initiating responses while most of the others are simply copying what the leaders say.

5. Information is secured about individuals through individual turns, which follow group tasks. The individual task provides definitive information about the ability of different students to respond to a task when there is no "support" from the group.

6. The assumption of Direct Instruction programs is that learning is not errorless and that students frequently make mistakes (even in response to the best designed presentations). Each program specifies the precise steps that the teacher is to take in correcting the more common errors. These specifications are scripted in a manner similar to the scripting of other parts of the lesson.

7. A final assumption in the communication between teacher and student is that the student will tend to enjoy the material and work on it more deliberately if the student is reinforced for good performance and hard work. Therefore, part of the communication involves praise and challenges, exhortations, and expressed amazement over the performance of the student. The idea is to present the work so that the learner will be able to master it in a way that impresses the teacher.

Beginning Reading

We will look at Lesson 57 of *DISTAR Reading* 1. The design of the lessons permits the teacher to complete one lesson a day in a 35-minute period (with all but the lowest performing group). For an average group of disadvantaged

Operational Description

children, therefore, Lesson 57 should be presented about three months after the beginning of school. (Average or bright children would not be placed in *DISTAR Reading* 1 but in the *DISTAR Fast Cycle* program, and they would be at the equivalent of about Lesson 160 after three months of school.)

If the teacher is not teaching a lesson a day but is teaching reasonably well, the children will be on an earlier lesson, such as Lesson 40, but they will be firm on what the teacher is teaching. If the teacher is going through a lesson a day but is not actually teaching to criterion, the teacher will be on Lesson 57; however, the children will not be able to perform on this lesson. When tested, they might place on Lesson 40. By knowing that the tasks presented in Lesson 57 are teachable within the timetable of a lesson a day, we are in a strong position to manage instruction.

The teacher is working with a group of eight children. They are arranged in two rows. The teacher sits very close to them. For the first task, the teacher displays a page of the presentation book (see Figure 1). The page shows a score box and a group of letters. The top row of the score box is headed with an *m*; the bottom row is headed with a mouthless face. The teacher says, "I'm smart. I bet I can beat you in a game. Here's the rule. When I touch a sound, you say it." Several children respond, "We're going to beat you."

The teacher prints a letter in the box and quickly touches under it. The children respond with the sound, "t." The teacher makes a tally mark in the bottom row of the score box, erases the *t*, and replaces it with *o*. Again the children respond in unison when the teacher touches under the letter.

Not all the children respond to the next letter, *a*. "Ho ho," the teacher says. "I got you on *a*." The teacher makes a tally mark in the *m* row. The game continues for about two minutes. At the completion of the game, there are 24 tallies

Figure 1

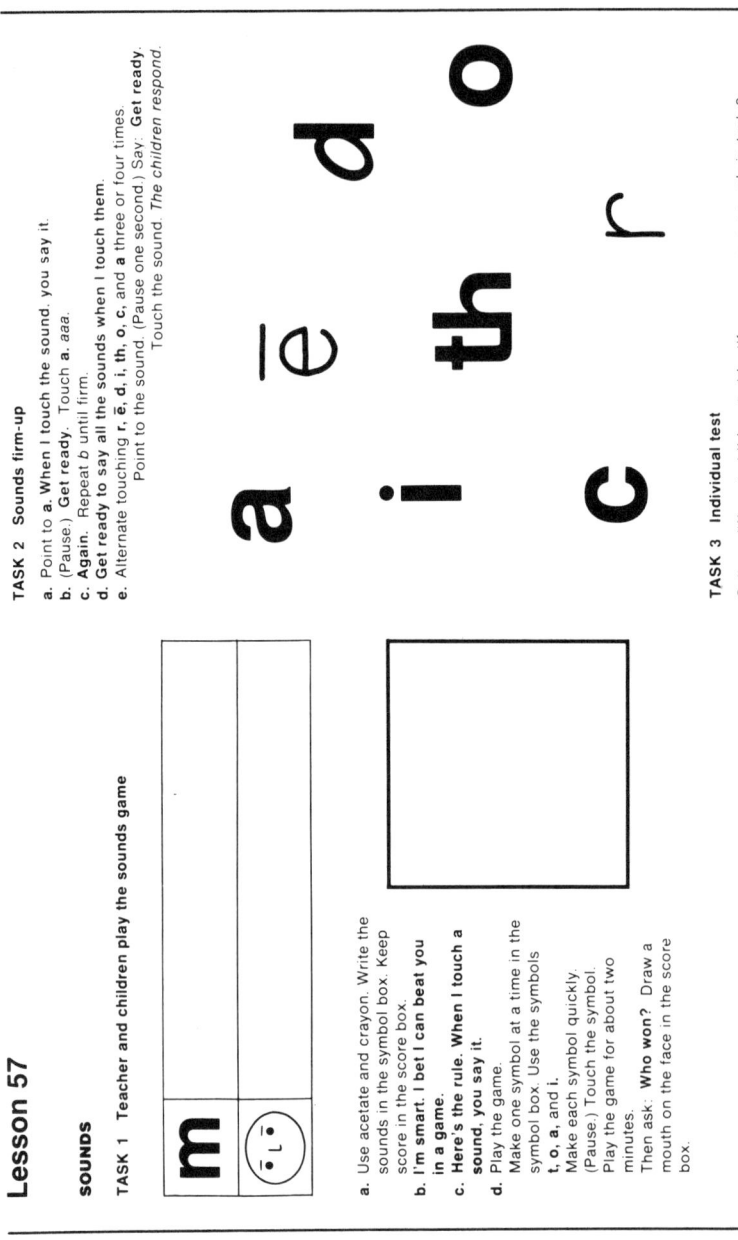

Operational Description

in the box. The children have 21. The teacher has three. "Who won?" the teacher asks.

"We did, we won," the children shout. The teacher makes a smiling mouth on the previously mouthless face. "You get a smiling face for knowing your sounds."

Very quickly, the teacher turns the page of the presentation book, displaying a column of words (see Figure 2). Each word is on an arrow, and each arrow has a ball on the left end and a point on the right. The teacher touches the ball of the first arrow (under the word *eat*).

"Sound it out. . . . Get ready." The teacher's finger quickly moves under the $\bar{e}$, pauses, and then moves under the *t* for an instant. The children say the sounds the finger points to. They say "ee" and then "t," without pausing between the sounds. (Say the word *eat* very slowly, holding the *e* until you say *t* and you will say it the way they sound it out.)

"Again," the teacher says, touching the ball of the arrow. Once more the finger moves, and the children sound out *eat*. The teacher then says, "Yes, what word?"

"Eat," the children respond.

Note: the letter *a* in "*eat*" is smaller than the others, and the children do not sound out small letters.

The next word is *sock*.

It, too, has a small letter (*k*). The teacher touches the ball of the arrow. "Sound it out. . . . Get ready," he or she says. His or her finger moves and stops under the *s*, under the *o*, and for an instant, under the *c*, as the children say the sounds "sssoooc" again without pausing between the sounds.

"Again," the teacher says, and traces the sounds with his or her finger as the children sound out the word. "Yes, what word?"

The same procedure is repeated for the other words on the page: *on, feet.*

The teacher then says, "That was a good job. Let's see who can read words on this page. Fran. . . ." The teacher points to

Figure 2

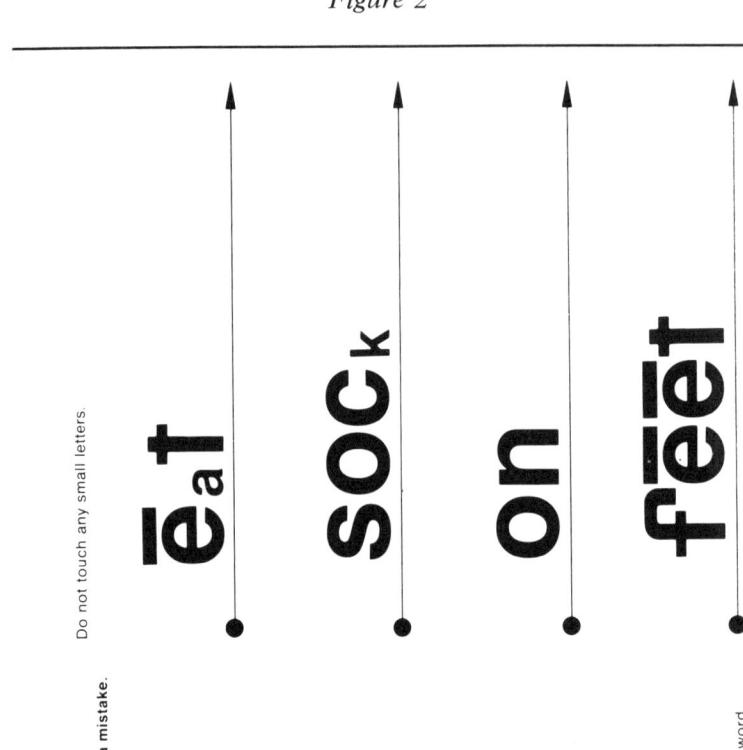

Operational Description 19

the arrow of the word "sock." "Sound it out. . . . Get ready . . . . Again . . . . Yes, what word? Good job, Fran." Other children receive individual turns on different words.

The sounding out operation is designed so that it leads the child as closely as possible to saying the word. There are no pauses between sounds, so the sounding out of a word is actually saying the word. The children, therefore, have far less trouble identifying the word after sounding it out. The traditional sounding out procedure has pauses between sounds: "rrr-uuuu-nnn." These pauses render the sounded out word quite different from the word "run" when it is spoken at a normal speaking rate.

The teacher quickly turns the page and repeats the decoding routine for six new words. The teacher then passes out workbooks to each child. The books are opened to the "take-home" for Lesson 57 (see Figure 3).

The teacher says, "Finger on the ball of the top arrow." He or she checks the children's fingers.

"Touch the first word . . . sound it out. Get ready." The teacher claps as the children sound out *it*. "Say it fast . . . Yes, what word? . . ."

"Touch the next word . . . sound it out. Get ready. . . ." The teacher claps as the children sound out "iiisss" (rhymes with hiss). "Say it fast."

"Iz," the children respond.

The sounding out is repeated for *on*. The teacher then praises the children and repeats the sounding out. The teacher then calls on individual children to read the words.

The teacher holds up a copy of the take-home and touches under the word *on*. "Everybody, this word is *on*. What word? . . . Yes, *on*. Remember that. We're going to read this story the fast way." The teacher points to the words *it is*. "I will read these the fast way." The teacher points to *on*. "When I touch this word, you are going to say . . ."

"On," the children respond.

Figure 3

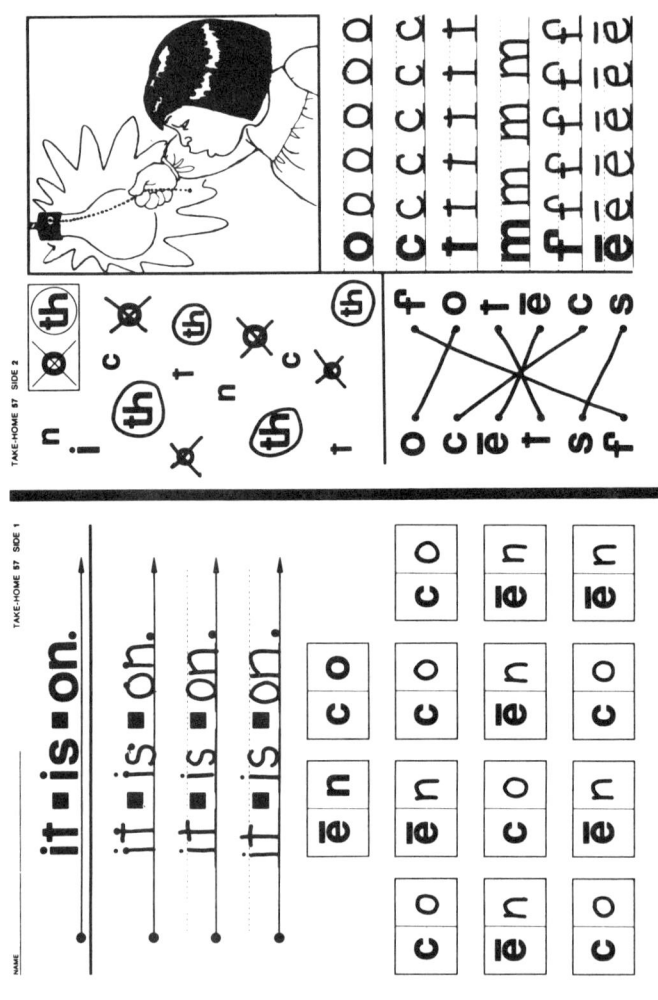

Figure 3 shows how the worksheet looks when it is completed by the child. The child has copied the sentence *it is on,* has filled in the empty boxes, followed the cross-out and circling instructions, joined matching letters, and copied the individual letters.

Operational Description

The teacher touches the ball of the arrow. "Reading the fast way...." The teacher's finger moves along the arrow. "It... is...." The teacher touches under *on*.

"On," some of the children say. "Good remembering," the teacher says. "Let's do it again." The procedure is repeated several times until all children perform.

"Listen," the teacher says, "It is on. You are going to see a picture of something and...." The teacher signals.

"It is on," the children respond.

"Turn your take-home over and look at the picture."

The children do. An illustration in the upper part of the reverse side shows a girl turning on a light. "Is something on in the picture?"

"Yes," the children respond. "That light is on."

"That light is pretty big, isn't it?... What would you do with a great big light bulb like that?"

"I got a big light," one child observes. "It is right near my window."

"Me too," another child says. Hands shoot up; children crowd around the teacher telling about their experiences with lights.

"Okay, that is good," the teacher says. "Now turn back to side one of your take-home." The teacher holds up his or her take-home. "...I am going to read the words the fast way... it... is... on... Again... it... is... on. Everybody, look at your take-home. Look for the word *it*. iiit. Everybody, point to iiit. Get your finger over the word iiit." The teacher checks the children. "Get ready to touch *it* when I clap... Get ready." The teacher claps.

"Good job.... Fingers up. Everybody look at the words in your story. Look for the word... *on*. Ooonnn... Everybody, point to ooonnn. Get your finger right over the word and get ready to touch... *on* when I clap... Get ready..." The teacher claps. The teacher repeats the pointing and touching for *it, on, on, it*.

The teacher praises the children and then says, "Everybody, you are going to finish this (Figure 3) take-home on your own. Let's go over the things you are going to do." The teacher points to the dotted words on the second line. "You are going to write the dotted words on this arrow. Then you are going to write those words on the other arrows."

The teacher points out the four other activities that the children will do independently. One involves writing letters in boxes. Two model boxes are provided: The children write the second letter in each of the 12 boxes below. The first letter for each is given. For example, $\bar{e}$ | |

Another activity is a cross-out game. There is a display of letters, predominantly *o* and *th*. A code near the top of the page shows the children that they are to cross out the sound *o* and circle the sound *th*.

A matching exercise requires the children to draw lines connecting every sound in Column 1 with the same sound in Column 2.

The final independent activity is a letter-writing task. The children practice printing o, c, t, m, f, and $\bar{e}$.

The children complete the worksheet activities in about 12 minutes. The teacher makes smiling faces at the top of each completed paper and asks each child, "Are you going to remember to read this story to your mama?" The children respond with affirmations, such as, "I do that all the time . . . I read it to my brother. He is in third grade but he don't read. . ."

The lesson is completed. For the teacher, it meant hard work. The teacher acted frisky and moved quickly to complete the activities in the allotted time. He or she had to rehearse his or her lines so that he or she could present the various tasks effectively, which is not always easy when pointing to something and trying to say the exact wording of the tasks. (Note that everything the teacher said in the

Operational Description

example above was part of the verbatim script for the lesson. There were no ad libs, not even with respect to the wording of the game examples at the beginning of the lesson.)

The control of teacher wording assures that:

1. Tasks are rarely failed because the children do not understand the instructions. The children learn exactly what each instruction calls for. The same instruction keys the same type of response (such as sounding out).

2. Modifications of instructions do not confuse the children. The earliest word-reading instruction in the program (Lesson 37) calls for the teacher to say, "Say it fast," after the word has been sounded out. The next word-reading instruction calls for the teacher to say, "Say it fast . . . Yes, what word?" The word-reading instructions in Lesson 57 (20 lessons after the first word-reading tasks) call for the teacher to say, "Yes, what word?" The children have been taught that "Say it fast" is the equivalent of "Yes, what word?" and the teaching has occurred effortlessly, perhaps without the teacher's knowledge.

3. The teacher can easily diagnose problems with any part of the operation because the operation is a sum of previously taught components. The teacher is familiar with these components, knowing how they were taught and how the children should respond to them.

4. The children learn that the same attack steps can be generalized to new words. For each, the children say the sounds, without pausing, and then say the word fast. They are not limited to the words that they "memorize" as sight words. The uniform operation (the same set of steps for each example of the operation) induces generalization, by showing the child that the same attack steps apply to all examples of a particular type.

The child cannot apply the sounding out operation to words that are irregularly spelled, such as *have, seat, he,* and *the.* The use of macrons (long lines over vowels) enables the child to read words like *he,* which is now a perfectly regular word. The joined letter **th** permits the word **there** to become regular. The small letters (not sounded) permit the word **we͏re** to be regular and not readily confused with **whe͏re** (which is also regular).

Since written English is not perfectly regular, irregulars must be introduced early. In Lesson 57, one such irregular is presented—the word *is*. Although it is sounded out as if it rhymes with *hiss,* it is not pronounced that way. The children are shown through the teacher's stipulation how to pronounce the word and that not all words are regular. Later, more complicated irregulars, such as *was* and *said* will be taught. No attempt is made to reduce these words to phonetic spelling. Virtually every word in DISTAR is spelled correctly. The macrons, joined letters, and small letters are simply used as guides to the pronunciation of letters. (This is a difference between ITA and DISTAR orthography. Children are never taught different spellings in DISTAR. The orthography is adjusted to *increase the application of the basic sounding out operation,* not to change basic spelling conventions.)

In addition to "sounding out" words, children are taught to attack words without sounding them out. This particular operation is often treated as a perfect mysterious process involving "sight words." The DISTAR approach is to account for "sight word" reading. Two exercises in Lesson 57 are designed for the transition from sounding out to "reading words the fast way." For one exercise, the teacher reads "It . . . is . . ." and the children read one word—*on*. The memory requirement for this task is small but the concept is important: every word retains its identity and can be remembered as a "unit" rather than a sum of parts. On subsequent lessons, the children will be responsible for increasingly difficult "reading the fast way" activities—remembering two words, remembering an entire sentence,

Operational Description

and finally reading words the fast way without sounding them out. The word-finding game, therefore, provides the children with relatively easy practice that reinforces the concept that each word retains its identity and can be referred to as a whole.

Note: Some linguists have objected to the teaching of individual sounds on the grounds these are "allophones" or different versions of the same sounds. The most variable are "stop sounds" such as *c, d, p,* and *t,* when they occur at the beginning of the word. (The *d* sound is different in each of these words: *d*ip, *d*ap, *d*op, *d*up because the sound must be produced in a way that permits a transition to the following letter.) DISTAR provides a solution to the linguist's dilemma by teaching a different attack for stop-sound-first words. To decode the word *tip,* the learner is first directed to the last part of the word, and sounds out *ip.* The teacher then points to the first letter and says, "This word rhymes with *ip* . . ." "Tip," the children respond and the allophone problem is solved. Of course, the rhyming skill is taught before the operation for stop-sound-first words is introduced.

As Lesson 57 illustrates, reading comprehension activities are taught in DISTAR. The children are taught that the printed statements predict. Images or pictures are based on what is written, not vice versa. When you read, "It is on," the picture will show "It is on." This order of events is the reverse of the traditional approach, which involves first looking at the picture and then reading the words (which happen to be consistent with the picture). The approach implies that the words are somehow a synonym for the "meaning" conveyed by the picture—a horrible misrule that is avoided in DISTAR by articulating the relationship between decoding and comprehension. Pictures may be derived from written statements; however, written statements cannot be derived from pictures. Later, comprehension activities will be taught with the same care that picture predictions are taught.

Activities are included in DISTAR to promote intrinsic motivation. For instance, the activities are designed so that the children are able to succeed (all children succeeding on all activities). Therefore, there is a reality-based reason for self-confidence and for enjoyment—success. There are tasks that provide payoffs for having learned different skills. For instance, the game permits the children to "beat the teacher" and to show how smart they are. By remembering what they are taught, they assure that they will continue to win these games. The fact that the children have performed successfully on the take-home sets the stage for additional practice and reinforcement of skills. The children can show off to their parents, who hopefully will respond by praising the children's achievement. Some activities are particularly enjoyable and the children look forward to them—such as the discussion about the picture.

Just as reading the fast way and comprehension activities are controlled, the transition from structured work to independent work is handled as part of the daily lesson. As skills are taught, they are integrated into the activities that students do on their own. In Lesson 57, students match sounds in two columns. Later, they will do a variation of the activity in which they match the words in one column with appropriate *word parts* in the facing column. In Lesson 57, they complete boxes that display letter pairs, such as $\bar{e}/n$. Later, they will deal with boxes that show a word and a picture. They will circle the picture if it corresponds to the word, or cross out the pictures that do not show the word, or complete the words.

Lesson 58 looks a lot like Lesson 57. A new sound is introduced in Lesson 58–$\bar{a}$–and the first activities deal with discriminating between the earlier taught *a* and the new sound $\bar{a}$. Following the work with sounds, the children read isolated words (sounding them out and identifying them); they read a little take-home "story" (Sit on it). They read the story the fast way, do picture comprehension activities, and word-finding and independent activities—copying, pairs, cross-out game matching, sound writing, and coloring the story picture. The examples change and new things are taught. But the new is *added*. Skills build in complexity; however, they do not usually disappear.

Our description of Lesson 57 shows the following features of Direct Instruction:

1. More than one thing is taught during a lesson.
2. What is taught is used in various contexts.
3. The teaching of each skill is very careful and is always considered within the context of all other skills that are taught. (There are no inconsistent operations or dead-end skills.)
4. Every aspect of the children's behavior is accounted for by the presentation.
5. The presentation is responsible for teaching, for motivating, for avoiding problems, for promoting generalizations, and for achieving increased "independence" and self-reliance.

The control that is exercised includes the teacher wording, examples, sequence of examples, distribution of practice, sequence of tasks, and distribution of tasks. Understandably, it is not easy to tell a teacher how to control all of these details without using a Direct Instruction program. The program typically will teach the teacher how to teach because it will show how to achieve such goals as "reading the fast way" or reading with comprehension.

The DISTAR programs do not provide the best possible way to teach any skill. The program is limited by the printed-page format, which prohibits the presentation of continuously-changing examples. Microcomputer presentations (with audio input and feedback) could potentially do a better job than DISTAR. Whether the presentation is processed through microcomputer or the printed page, however, the program will be complicated if it is to be efficient. It must assure that a variety of skills is taught during a lesson and that each of these skills develops from day to day. It must anticipate particular problems and buttress against these. And the program must teach the *preskills for every operation.* The operation of sounding out words implies the preskills that are taught before Lesson 57 in *DISTAR Reading* 1. The children are taught how to "say it fast." This teaching is first conducted with verbally presented words, beginning with the easiest type in Lesson 1: "Listen: Motor–boat. Say it fast. . . . Listen: Ice–cream. Say it fast . . ."

The children are also taught that it is possible to "say the sounds" of verbally presented words. "Listen: Say the sounds in *am.* What word? . . . Say the sounds in *am.*" The children are taught to combine the sounding out of verbally presented words with saying the word fast. "Listen: iiifff. Say it with me: iiifff. Say it fast . . . . What word?" Note that this task contains nearly all of the ingredients of the word-reading procedure for words like *if:*

"Sound it out. Get ready: (iiiifff).

Say it fast: (if)."

The children are taught to identify letters as sounds, starting with *m* and *a* in Lesson 1 and proceeding at the rate of about one new sound every three lessons.

If the teaching is careful, virtually all children can be taught the component or prerequisite skills. Since each subsequent teaching step involves using variations of these previously taught skills, the learning of more complex skills is therefore guaranteed. With adequate care, all children can read.

Equations

Our second look at Direct Instruction occurs in a fifth-grade classroom. The teacher does not work with a small group but with the entire class. The exercise comes from the E-B Press equations program (tryout edition). The lesson is similar to the *DISTAR Reading* 1 lesson in basic design:

(a) all tasks are specified, including the teacher wording for all steps;

(b) for newly introduced skills, the teacher takes the students through an operation, with all steps overt;

(c) later skills are "faded" so the students carry out the steps without direction from the teacher;

(d) the operation is a sum of skills that have been taught; and

(e) the operation applies to a wide range of problems.

Rather than going through an entire lesson, we will look at the presentation of one problem from Lesson 20. The problem comes as the third activity of this lesson, following the teacher-directed workbook problem. The teacher, who is standing in front of the chalkboard, presents the next problem:

"I will tell you a problem and we will work it on the board. You figure out what two things you are dealing with. Listen: How many bags of nails would Bob need to make three chairs. What two things are you dealing with?"

Students: "Bags and chairs."

The teacher writes on the board: B

C

Teacher: "How many bags of nails does Bob use to make three chairs? What do I write next to B and C?"

Students: "Box and three."

The teacher writes on the board: B ☐

C 3

Teacher: "Listen: How many bags does Bob use if he used two bags to make five chairs? What do I write for B and C?"

Students: "Two and five."

The teacher writes: B ☐ 2

C 3 5

Teacher: "Tell me how to write the problem. Get ready."
Students: "How many over three equals two over five."
The teacher draws in lines and sign: $\frac{B}{C} \frac{\square}{3} = \frac{2}{5}$

Teacher: "Which way do the arrows go?"
Students: Point right to left.
The teacher draws the arrows: $\frac{B}{C} \frac{\square \leftarrow 2}{3 \leftarrow 5}$

Teacher: "Where do you work first in this problem?"
Students: "On the bottom."
Teacher: "Read that problem."
Students: "Five times some fraction equals three."
Teacher: "Tell me the fraction you multiply the five by?"
Students: "Three-fifths."
The teacher writes: $\frac{B}{C} \frac{\square \leftarrow (\frac{3}{5})2}{3 \leftarrow (\frac{3}{5})5}$

Teacher: "Figure out the answer."
Students mentally multiply two times three-fifths.
Teacher: "How many bags would Bob need to make three chairs if he used two bags to make five chairs?"
Students: "Six-fifths."
The teacher writes the answer.

Before proceeding, take a piece of paper and work the problem as the teacher does. (Follow the description above and write the things the teacher writes for each response.)

The problem-solving strategy assumes that the students have been taught responses before they encountered this particular problem. For instance, the teacher asks them to "figure out the answer." To figure it out, the students must carry out a number of steps. At one time, these steps were specified as overt acts. In the problem above, however, the steps have been "faded" so that the students carry them out without teacher guidance.

Operational Description

The justification for the somewhat elaborate attack on the problem is that simple variations of this same attack will lead to solutions of many problems. Here are some story problems that are typically not understood by all but those students who have "aptitude" for arithmetic.

1. An elm tree is 20 feet tall and its shadow is 13 feet long. If an oak is 17 feet tall, how long is its shadow?
2. If seven men are needed to carry two yards of concrete, how many yards could 11 men carry?
3. How many houses could a crew build in five days, if they can build two houses in seven days?
4. During a sale, everything is reduced by the same percentage. Before the sale, pants were 11 dollars and hats were eight. If hats are five dollars during the sale, how much are pants?
5. If ten percent of the dirt weighs 13 tons, how much would nine percent of the dirt weigh?
6. If a man travels four miles in five hours, how far will he travel in seven hours?

The student who is provided with a method of solving ratio problems is able to solve all these types of problems. The student is also able to work simple, formal problems such as:
$$5r = 17$$
$$3r = \square$$

This is simply another ratio problem. It can be written this way:
$$\frac{5}{3} = \frac{17}{\square}$$

That all these problems are the same may not be at all obvious to the reader (who may have learned that they are basically different in form). All the problems are the same, however, and the same attack leads to a solution of all of them.

This situation is somewhat similar to the word-reading

operation. In both cases, we wanted the same operation to apply to the widest possible range of examples. The solution to the word-reading problem was to change the orthography so that more words would become regular. The solution for the equations problem is *to design an attack that holds for all ratio problems.*

The ratio problem: $\dfrac{7}{3} = \dfrac{\Box}{4}$

indicates that we will multiply 7/3 by some fraction *that equals one.* The top number and the bottom of this fraction will be the same. When we multiply by this fraction, we will create a fraction with a denominator of four.

To figure the fraction of one, we first draw an arrow toward the empty box. This arrow shows us which way we will multiply: $\dfrac{7 \rightarrow}{3 \rightarrow} = \dfrac{\Box}{4}$

We also draw another arrow on the bottom. Both arrows go in the same direction.

We can't figure out the top number (because of the box). Therefore, we must work on the bottom, and figure out what we multiply three by to change it into four. The answer is 4/3. It can be figured out with the following operation:

$$3(\quad) = 4$$

The problem says that we multiply three by some fraction to change it into four. If we don't know what to multiply three by, we first change the left side of the equation into *one.* To do this, we multiply by the reciprocal of three:

$$3\left(\tfrac{1}{3}\right) = 4$$

The sides are not equal because there is one on the left and four on the right. But now we can easily figure out what is needed in the parentheses to make the sides equal. One times what number equals four? Four. So we multiply by four on the left:

$$3 \left(\frac{1}{3} \cdot \frac{4}{1} \right) = 4$$

The answer is inside the parentheses: We multiplied three by 4/3 to change it into four.

Note that this analysis permits the learner to figure out what to multiply any value by to change it into any other value.

If we multiply by 4/3 on the bottom of the original problem:

$$\frac{7 \longrightarrow}{3 \left(\frac{4}{3} \right) \longrightarrow} = \frac{\square}{4}$$

we must multiply by 4/3 on the top. (If we don't, we won't multiply by one.)

$$\frac{7 \left(\frac{4}{3} \right) \longrightarrow}{3 \left(\frac{4}{3} \right) \longrightarrow} = \frac{\square}{4}$$

Multiplying seven by 4/3 yields 28/3, which is the answer.

A single problem solution permits the learner to handle all basic ratio problems. Furthermore, the solution is not mysterious but is based on demonstrable principles. The approach replaces intuition with logical procedures that permit a straightforward attack on any problem. And, perhaps most important, the skills that the learner is required to master before applying the problem-solving strategy to various problems are reduced substantially.

They are:

1. The learner is taught to discriminate whether fractions are equal to one or not equal to one.

2. The learner "proves" or demonstrates that a fraction such as 3/3 is equal to one.

3. The learner is taught that multiplying by one does not change the amount you start with and that this rule holds for any fraction of one (eight multiplied by 5/5 equals eight because the top number gets eight times bigger, but so does the bottom number).

4. Next, the learner is taught to change any fraction into one by multiplying. $\frac{4}{3}(\quad) = 1$

The answer is 3/4. When multiplied by 4/3, the top equals 12 and the bottom equals 12.

5. The learner is taught to solve any problem of this form: "One times what fraction equals 5/6?" Or, "One times what fraction equals nine over one?" Or, "One times what fraction equals A over B?" $\frac{3}{4}(\quad) = \frac{7}{8}$

6. The learner is taught the key operation of changing any number into any other number by multiplying.

With these skills, the learner is ready to apply the full-blown strategy (such as the one presented in Lesson 20 of the equations program) to a variety of problems.

Summary

The two examples of Direct Instruction are different in many ways. Their differences derive from the fact that each application teaches dramatically different skills. As we will see in the following chapters, the structure of what is taught is the primary guideline for designing Direct Instruction. The examples of Direct Instruction are the same, however, in important ways. Both account for everything the learner must be taught. Both try to achieve this learning in a highly efficient way. The efficiency may not be apparent with the application of one problem (or with the reading of one word). Repeated applications show that the same set of steps is involved with each application. If the same steps lead to the solution of apparently diverse problems, these problems must be the same. Once this generalized understanding of the structure of problems has been induced, the learner is in a position to experiment, to make up varied applications, and

Operational Description

to test the limits. The learner is not frightened of a problem such as: $\dfrac{2}{12} = \dfrac{\square}{P}$

Direct Instruction does not treat generalizations as strange properties of the learner. They are predictable, manipulable products that are guaranteed if the teaching is based on sound instructional principles.

III.

DESIGN FORMAT

Introduction

This chapter presents the Direct Instruction analysis of concepts. The analysis implies how to teach virtually anything. However, the treatment of many important topics is sketchy. The chapter places strongest emphasis on the *initial teaching* of concepts—not so much on the expansion or application of what is taught. The reason is that teachers typically fail in understanding how to demonstrate what a concept is, how it works, and what kind of responses are associated with it. Applications and expansions are vital to successful instructional sequences; however, these applications are more easily achieved than the initial-teaching sequences.

The analysis is based on the idea that there are only three types of basic discriminations and that every complex activity is composed entirely of combinations of these discriminations:

1. *Choice-response discriminations.* The task presents the choice of responses the learner is to produce: Tell me if it gets wider or if it doesn't get wider.

2. *Production-response discriminations.* The task tells the learner to produce or create a response that is not given in the task: What is this?

3. *Sentence-relationship discriminations.* The examples of this discrimination always involve a sentence.

These discriminations may be *taught* by using variations of a formula for communicating with the learner through a sequence of examples.

The communication formula specifies how to design a sequence of examples so that it is consistent with *only one possible interpretation.*

This basic communication goal—communicating so that the presentation is consistent with only one interpretation—is applied to the teaching of complex attack strategies as well as to the teaching of basic discriminations. Complex strategies consist of chains of basic discriminations. The chains are designed so that everything the learner does is *overt.* When it is overt, the teacher can observe what the learner does and assure that the learner is taking the component steps that are needed to achieve the appropriate outcome. Once the chain has been mastered, the learner is taught to use it in a covert manner.

Communication

Direct Instruction begins with the idea that the learner is a magnificent piece of machinery, capable of learning just about anything we wish to teach—if we are empathic in our presentation. To be empathic, we must try to look at things from the standpoint of the naive learner, not from that of the sophisticated teacher of instructional design. We must avoid the trap of face validity. This trap comes about when we fail to consider alternative interpretations. For example, we may note that an act of hugging a child is an act of love. If we conclude that hugging a child *communicates* love to the child, we would fall into the trap of face validity. The conclusion is based on lexical gymnastics. An actual, concrete hug may communicate confinement, even hatred, to a particular learner. Traditional educational approaches are characterized by much face-validity reasoning. The teacher talks about the character, Joy, in the beginning reading

Design Format

program before reading the word, Joy, below the picture. This act may be classified as an act of "comprehension" or "arousing interest." The teacher insists that the act, therefore, promotes comprehension or arouses interest. In fact, the act may have the exact opposite effect. It may imply to the child that words are decoded by attending to pictures or to the verbal scenario that the teacher provides in connection with these pictures. Both messages are dangerous; yet both are implied by the teacher's presentation as clearly as the message that the teacher insists is being conveyed.

Direct Instruction begins with the idea that it takes much more than good intentions to "teach" or demonstrate what you set out to teach or demonstrate. The fact that *we* can classify an act as one that "involves reading comprehension" or one that "explains quantum mechanics" or one that "involves discovery" does not mean that the learner will derive this message from the act. The intended message will be conveyed to the learner only if the act is designed so that NO OTHER INTERPRETATION IS POSSIBLE.

Analysis of Concepts or Discriminations

Building a program involves orchestrating a number of activities at once. It involves complex attack strategies or routines that permit the learner to solve a particular class of problems or to read words of a particular type. These strategies are composed of more basic building blocks, which are concepts and discriminations. These concepts and discriminations must be taught before the more elaborate strategies are taught. Teaching these concepts involves doing more than providing a brief, concise communication with the learner. Teaching involves two phases—the first of which shows precisely how the concept or discrimination works, while the second expands the concept and provides practice with it in a wide range of contexts.

The major point in program design, however, is that what

is taught is used. Conversely, if a concept or discrimination is needed for a complex application, it is first taught.

Let us say that we wish to teach children the idea that when the stoplight is red, they are not to cross the street. This objective presents the various discriminations that should be pre-taught. Furthermore, the objective clarifies the particular meanings that the learner must be taught. The objective refers to *red,* but the particular meaning that is needed is quite clear. It is the color red, not the other meanings that may be found in a dictionary (such as "I'm so angry, I see red."). The specific meanings of the other things referred to in the objective—street, crossing the street, and the idea that if the light is red you don't cross—are also clear. By first identifying objectives, we can avoid many problems in trying to design instructional sequences. We will not try to use survey or statistical information as the basis for determining which discriminations should be taught (or which meanings of particular words). For instance, if it happened that young children learned the color blue more readily than red, we would not change our objective to teach children something about blue lights and crossing streets. We certainly would not teach discriminations that the learner is incapable of learning; however, we would not use spurious guides, such as normative data, to determine what the learner should learn. We begin with an objective, something judged important or useful for the learner to master. We then teach whatever component skills or discriminations are incorporated in this objective.

Discriminations

The analysis of a concept or discrimination involves two aspects. The first is obvious. We must analyze the structure of the concept that is to be taught. If we are to teach the color red, we must first analyze what red is and what it is not. Perhaps we don't have to concern ourselves with the most precise theoretical aspects of red; however, we should know what the range of questionable redness is (the range in which there is not perfect consensus among knowledgeable people) and the range of safe redness (the range that presents no problems). Similarly, if we wish to teach the learner what a "vowel" is, we must analyze the concept *vowel* to see the various problems (Is the *w* sound sometimes a vowel sound?) and understand the structure of what we are to teach. If we know what red is, we are obviously in a better position to teach the discrimination.

But understanding the structure of the discrimination is not enough. We must understand how to convey this structure to the learner through examples. After all, this type of communication is what will ultimately take place, and (as we noted above) the communication makes a potentially big difference in the message received by the learner. Will the message actually communicate the structure of the discrimination to the learner? Or, will it convey some unintended message? If the communication is designed so that only one message or interpretation is possible, the communication will teach what it is designed to teach. If it is poorly designed, however, it may fail.

Sameness-Difference

The basic idea behind all communication that involves examples is that if examples are treated in the same way, they are the same in some way. If we call two objects the same name—"Blurb"—the learner who receives this communication assumes that there is something the same about both the objects. This sameness, this observable quality, is the basis for the label.

If we treat things in the same way, they are the same in some way. It follows that if we treat things differently, they are different in some way. If we label one thing as a *blurb* and another as *not-blurb,* we are implying that the difference in the label is based on observable differences in the object.

This basic sameness-difference game is usually (but not necessarily) played with words. "Red," we say as we point to one object. "It is red." We then point to another object and say, "It is not red." The fact that our response to the two objects is different signals the learner to attend to some structural difference in the examples. What features or properties does one of the objects have that are not shared by the other object and that could be the basis for labeling the objects differently?

When we engage in sameness-difference communication with the learner, we may not always communicate what we wish to communicate. Let us say, for instance, that we present two objects to the naive learner, a red card and a black truck. We indicate that the card is "red" and that the truck is "not red." The learner, therefore, must hypothesize about why one object is called "red" and another "not red." The difference in labels implies that the examples are different in a relevant way. The problem is that they are different in many, many ways. One object is flat and the other is three-dimensional. One object has moving parts and the other doesn't. One is familiar as a "truck" and the other isn't. One has a surface feature (a color) that the other doesn't have. And so forth. Which difference is an appropriate basis for *red*? If the learner selects the wrong difference, the learner may conclude that *red* is another word for card, that *red* is something flat, that *red* is something roughly square, etc.

The point: *A presentation of examples is not automatically consistent with only one interpretation.* If it is consistent with more than one interpretation, however, our communication is faulty. An undesired interpretation (such as the interpretation that *red* is another word for card) is as likely to be learned as the intended interpretation. *And both are perfectly consistent with the presentation of examples.*

The solution to this communication problem is to design

Design Format

the presentation in a way that rules out all but one interpretation. This process becomes a game of logic, something like a game of chess. There are certain procedures that you must follow; however, for given "problems," you may find yourself in unique situations.

One of the most basic procedures that we follow is that we present more than one example of a discrimination. (To present the example, we show it and label it in some way to establish a basis for demonstrating which other examples are treated in the same way.) More than one example is needed because it is impossible to present a single example of anything that is consistent with only one interpretation. Try to present a concrete example of something that is only black (an example with no features other than blackness). Or, try to present something that is only a cup (something that could not be interpreted as anything but *cup*). Experiments with different discriminations will reveal that it is impossible to present a single example of anything that conveys a single interpretation. In fact, a single example always conveys thousands of possible interpretations.

Similar procedures dictate that we must show more than one positive example of a given discrimination, if we expect to communicate the range of variation that is possible among positives. Also, we must show negative examples of a concept, if we expect to communicate what it is that changes a particular positive example into a negative.

Juxtaposition of Examples

Because we must present more than one example to communicate about any discrimination, a new variable is introduced into the communication—the juxtaposition of examples. If the learner's attention is directed first to one example and then to another, the ordering of these examples becomes important in conveying specific information to the learner.

Let's say that we present the examples of slanted in the first column of Figure 4.

Note that the examples are not presented on paper to the learner. To present the examples as the teacher would show them to the learner, take a pencil and hold it in a vertical position to create Example 1. As you hold the pencil in that position, say, "Not slanted." Then rotate the pencil to create Example 2. Hold the pencil stationary and tell the learner, "Slanted." Rotate the pencil so that it is almost vertical, stop, and tell the learner, "Slanted."

The learner would most probably not be able to note the difference between Example 1 and Example 3. The reason is that the examples *are not juxtaposed* in a way that demonstrates difference. *To demonstrate difference, we juxtapose examples that are labeled differently and are highly similar.* The second column of Figure 4 shows the appropriate juxtaposition of the examples. Take your pencil and present this sequence. You will observe that although the difference between Example 1 and Example 2 is slight, this difference is quite perceptible when Example 2 follows Example 1 with no interruptions. We can see how the examples are different because *only one change occurs between Example 1 and Example 2.* That change is a slight shift in orientation of the object. However, that shift is demonstrated to be relevant because the first orientation of the object is labeled "Not slanted" and the second is labeled "Slanted." The examples are treated differently, signaling a relevant difference in the examples. If the only difference is the slight change in orientation, the slight change in orientation must be the feature that caused the change in the label. The learner is shown *exactly* what causes "slantedness."

Continuous Conversion

The context in which very small differences are most

Design Format

Figure 4

Examples	Teacher Wording	Examples	Teacher Wording
1.	"Not slanted."		"Not slanted."
2.	"Slanted."		"Slanted."
3.	"Slanted."		"Slanted."

obvious is the one that you used when presenting the examples above. That context is called continuous conversion of examples. One example is converted into the next example with no interruptions. The conversion permits the learner to see the precise difference or change that is created. Furthermore, the conversion requires less memory on the learner's part. Let us say that we presented the same three examples of "slanted" that appear in the second column of Figure 4 as non-continuous examples. Here is how we would do that: We would present Example 1 (pencil vertical) and we would label the example "Not slanted." We would now put the pencil down at our side. Pick it up again and present Example 2, holding the pencil in a very slightly slanted orientation. Again we would label the example, "Slanted." The examples are not continuous because we did not convert one example into another. Instead, we started over and created the second example "from scratch." If you present the sequence in the second column as a series of non-continuous examples, you will observe that the difference between Example 1 and Example 2 is again imperceptible (or, at best, very difficult to perceive). Why? Because we are no longer juxtaposing Example 2 with Example 1. We are juxtaposing Example 2 with an event that shows the pencil at your side. The sequence of examples therefore demands far more sophisticated skills from the learner. The learner must construct a detailed mental picture of the first example and then compare this picture with the second example to determine any differences. There is only one slight difference between the examples, so it is unlikely that the learner would register this difference.

The point: *Continuous conversion of examples is the most effective way to present a series of examples,* because continuous conversion of examples does not require attention to *all* features of the example, merely those that change from example to example.

Design Format

We cannot present all concepts through continuous conversion of examples. However, we should try to approximate continuous conversion as much as possible, particularly when working with naive learners. We should recognize that comparison of two static examples requires far more skill than comparison of an example that undergoes dynamic changes.

Principles of Juxtaposition

Douglas Carnine has done a number of studies that investigate whether the logical analysis of communicating through examples predicts the performance of learners. The Appendix provides a summary of studies that relate to the kind of positive and negative examples selected for demonstrating a concept and to the juxtaposition of examples. These studies show that indeed the logical analysis predicts learning outcomes. The studies imply that the instructional designer should understand the facts of communicating through examples, particularly the facts about juxtaposition of examples. We can express these facts as four important principles about achieving different communication effects.

1. To show the most about a concept with the fewest possible examples, design all examples so they share the greatest number of features.
2. To show the most about differences, juxtapose examples that are minimally different and label each differently.
3. To show the most about sameness, juxtapose examples that are maximally different and label each the same.
4. To test the learner, juxtapose examples that bear no predictable relationship.

Principle 1 suggests that if we want to introduce a concept, such as "getting bigger," we can demonstrate the most about it through the fewest number of examples, if all examples involve the maximum number of features that are the same. Obviously, each example will be different. Some will show something getting bigger; others will show something that is not getting bigger. What Principle 1 tells us, however, is that if the first example of getting bigger in the sequence involves a balloon, all examples in the sequence involve the same balloon. If the first example shows a hand and a mouth on the balloon, all examples in the sequence show the mouth and hand on the balloon. The only difference from example to example is whether the balloon gets bigger.

When only one difference occurs from example to example, the learner can be shown most articulately how the changes affect the labels that we give the examples. The learner can therefore construct something of a mental map of how the concept works.

Principle 2, which we have already discussed, suggests that very small differences in examples provide the learner with the greatest information about difference, if these examples are juxtaposed and are labeled differently. (Only one small change occurs from example to example; however, the label changes. Therefore, this small change in the example must be the cause of the label change.)

Principle 3 is the opposite of Principle 2. To show how examples are the same, we juxtapose greatly different examples; however, these are labeled in the same way. Therefore, the differences are not sufficient to cause a change in label. Instead, these differences mark the range of acceptable variation for the discrimination.

Principle 4 is based on an assumption that we will do more than tell the learner and show the learner. We will also test to see whether the appropriate interpretation has been received by the learner. This test should be designed in a way that provides unambiguous results about the learner's reception. Therefore, it should contain a sufficient number of examples, and the juxtapositions should not provide a hint about the

Design Format 49

next example. (If examples in the group of test items were arranged so that they followed a pattern, such as: positive, positive, negative, negative, positive . . . . the learner could perform correctly on any test items without actually attending to the items. The items, therefore, should be juxtaposed so that no pattern is evident.)

Sequences for Teaching Discriminations

The principles above would be applied to the teaching of any discrimination, because any discrimination that we select must be demonstrated through examples, and examples must be juxtaposed. We wouldn't be able to construct a single format that would permit us to teach any discrimination, because not all discriminations have the same structure or are of the same "type." We must, therefore, have different sequences for discriminations of different types.

Before we classify these types, however, let's begin by showing what an initial-teaching sequence looks like when it is designed in accordance with the four principles above. Such a sequence appears in Figure 5. The brackets show the examples that are based on each principle. All examples are based on Principle 1; therefore, the bracket labeled '1' spans all examples. The bracket labeled '2' shows that there are two sets of examples designed to show the learner the difference between the positive examples of wider and negative examples. These examples are minimally different from each other but are labeled differently. Bracket 3 indicates that sameness of positive examples is conveyed through three examples. These examples differ maximally from each other; however, all are labeled in positives. Bracket 4 shows that after the learner has been shown something about the difference and something about the sameness of the *wider* examples, the learner is tested on an unpredictable order of examples.

To gain the most understanding of this sequence, create it. Start with your hands about six inches apart and say, "Watch

Figure 5

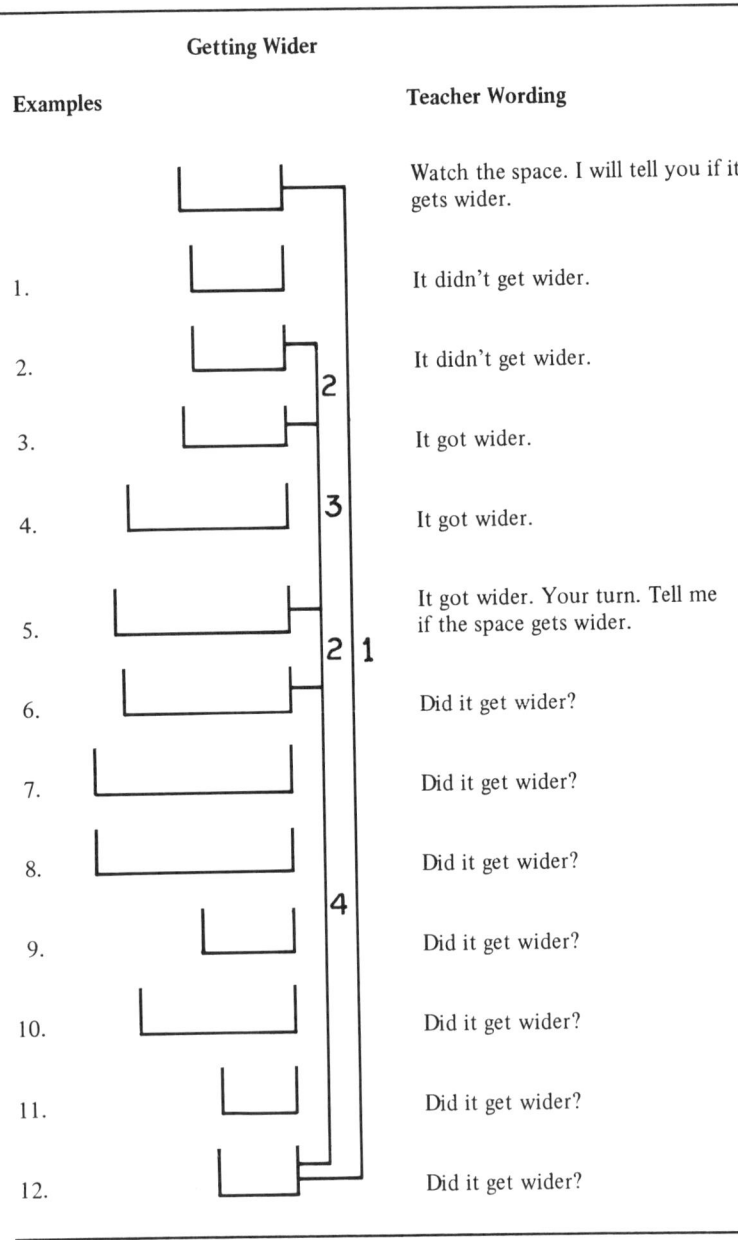

Design Format 51

the space. I will tell you if it gets wider." Then move the right hand in slightly and label the example. "It didn't get wider." Hold both hands stationary and say, "It didn't get wider." Move your right hand out slightly and say, "It got wider." Create the rest of the examples in this way. Move fairly quickly with no delays between examples. Run the sequence two or three times and think about the responses of the naive learner. By the time you have presented Example 2, the learner knows that whatever "wider" means, it can't mean hands and it can't mean merely movement. (You have shown hands in two examples that did not get wider, and you have moved your hand to create one example.) With the presentation of Example 3, the learner is shown that a particular type of movement *is* an example of getting wider. Additional examples are needed to reinforce this notion and to confirm the idea that it is labeled "getting wider" whether it moves a very slight amount or a great amount and that it is getting wider whether the absolute distance between the hands is relatively large or small. However, the sequence induces the idea of what *causes* something to be labeled "getting wider" very quickly.

Structure and Sequences

One of the most difficult notions for someone not familiar with Direct Instruction is the idea of same-structure-same-sequence. The sequence above is a comparative. All comparatives have exactly the same basic structure as *getting wider.* All require a comparison. (In the sequence above, the comparison is achieved by telling how the current example compares to the one that had been presented immediately before it.) All are binary discriminations. (Something either gets wider or it doesn't get wider.) Because of the structural sameness, we can teach *all* comparatives through the same format or arrangement of examples. The concept *more porous* could be taught using the same juxtapositions as those in the sequence for teaching *getting wider. Getting heavier* could be taught in the same way. So could *higher frequency,* or *greater intensity.* The sequence that is capable of showing the structure of one comparative is capable of showing the structure for all. This doesn't mean, of course, that we would use space between the hands to teach *heavier.* For *heavier,* we might place the learner's hand on a table and press down on his or her palm. The examples, however, would parallel those of *getting wider.* The first would be a starting point, perhaps pressing down with six pounds. "Feel this. I will tell you if it gets heavier." The next would be slightly negative, perhaps reducing the pressure to five pounds. "It didn't get heavier." Now the pressure stays the same for Example 2. "It didn't get heavier." And a minimum difference for Example 3. Slightly more pressure. "It got heavier." And so forth. Every single comparative could be presented through the same form. Furthermore, the form is capable of *teaching,* which means that the learner would always know what the concept is after successfully performing the sequence.

Although every comparative could be taught through the same basic form, many aspects of given sequences are arbitrary. To teach the concept *getting wider,* we used the space between our hands. Virtually all learners could learn from this presentation. However, the use of hands is arbitrary. We could use any device or object that is capable of creating examples called for by the principles of juxtaposition. We could use a door (the same door for all examples). Similarly, we might use actual weights for teaching *getting heavier* (making sure that the learner didn't watch the weights).

The statement that every comparative can be taught through the same form doesn't mean that we would teach the learner various comparatives using precisely the same patterns of examples as that of the sequence above—negative, negative, positive, positive, positive, negative . . . . The learner would tend to memorize the pattern and therefore might not learn to attend to the examples we present. To avoid this problem, we would use alternative forms for teaching a concept. The primary alternative form begins with three positives rather than two negatives. Also, the arrangement of examples in the test part of the sequence changes from sequence to sequence. Whether the sequence begins with positives or negatives, however, the sequence would be designed to show which changes and which features cause an example to become a positive example of the concept or a negative example. If the sequence achieves this goal, it is an effective initial-teaching sequence. It does not provide the learner with information about the full range of contexts in which the concept occurs. It simply shows what features are essential for the concept, and it does so quite quickly.

Although it may take the instructional designer some time to create a sequence that effectively follows a form, the naive learner could probably complete the sequence above in less than a minute. The learner would now be ready to see how this kernel concept applies to other situations.

Three Basic Sequences

Choice-Response Discriminations

The discrimination *getting wider* is a choice-response discrimination. This means that the task presented with each test example presents a choice of responses. The task mentioned the discrimination, "Did it *get wider*?" We could substitute this task for other choice-response tasks, such as, "Tell me wider or not wider." In any case, the same task would have been presented with all test examples, and the task would be designed so that it presented the learner with a choice of responses.

All choice-response discriminations can be taught through

variations of the same form sequence. Included would be discriminations ranging from *dendritic pattern* and *higher pitched* to *wet* and *over*. All comparatives are choice-response discriminations (*faster, more certain, less ambiguous*, etc.). So are all non-comparatives that involve only a single dimension. (If you can change a positive example of a concept into a negative or vice versa by changing only one dimension, the concept is a single-dimensional concept.) Positional words and many adjectives (red, stubborn) are single-dimensional words. The primary test of the choice-response discrimination is whether the task presents a choice to the learner. "Is this a vein or an artery?" The question implies a choice-response sequence. And all choice-response sequences are constructed in basically the same way as the model shown for the discrimination *getting wider*. For non-comparatives, the sequence would start out differently than in the *getting wider* sequence. The comparative sequence begins with a starting point example that is neither positive nor negative. The purpose of this example is to provide a basis for judging the example that follows. A starting point example has no place in a sequence that teaches a non-comparative, such as *moving from, second*, or *on*, because these concepts are non-comparatives. The first example in the sequence is, therefore, either positive or negative.

Other differences in the structure of various choice-response discriminations dictate minor adjustments in the sequence. However, three types of juxtaposition patterns occur in all sequences—those that demonstrate how examples are different, those that show how positives are the same, and those that test on a range of positives and negatives. Also, all examples in the sequence are designed so they are the same as each other in the greatest number of ways. (When the examples are designed in this way, the number of variables is reduced and the probability is increased that the learner will attend to relevant features of the examples.)

Design Format

Production-Response Discriminations

Production responses are not drastically different from choice-response sequences. Instead of asking the learner to respond to choices that we present through tasks, the production-response sequence asks the learner to produce responses. For instance, the teacher presents different addition problems and asks the same question about each: "What's the answer?" The learner produces different responses for different problems. Or, the teacher presents a list of verb words and says for each, "Say the past tense of this word." Again, the learner produces different responses for different examples.

There are no negative examples for the production-response sequence, because the instructions require the learner to produce positives. Here are some different instructions: "What's the predicate of that sentence?" "Where is the ball?" "Tell me the answer."

The simplest type of production-response sequence is one that teaches "noun" concepts. Things that are identified with noun labels are not single-dimensional concepts but multi-dimensional. This means that we could change a positive example of shoe into a negative by changing any of a number of features—the height of the uppers, the material, or by removing parts, such as the sole or the uppers.

A sequence for teaching nouns does not try to show extremely small, minimum differences, because there is no clear dividing line between a shoe and something that is not a shoe. (This point can be easily demonstrated by having a group of knowledgeable adults judge whether or not various articles of footwear are shoes. Agreement is far less than perfect.) Also, a sequence for teaching nouns does not present continuous conversion of examples. Perhaps the biggest difference between a sequence for teaching nouns and one for teaching choice-response concepts is that the noun sequence uses a different task form. For each test example in the sequence, the task would be: "What is this?" or "What kind of a _____ is this?" Note that the learner does not respond by referring to negatives.

The noun sequence follows the same principles of juxtaposition that govern choice-response sequences. Differences between the new discrimination and other somewhat similar discriminations are shown. Examples are used to show how various instances of the new discrimination are the same. And test examples follow the demonstration examples. Figure 6 illustrates a noun sequence for teaching the discrimination of black oak leaves from maple and white oak leaves. Note that maple leaves and white oak leaves have already been taught to the learner.

For some production-response concepts, a different strategy is needed to show the learner how the concept operates. These concepts are called single-transformation concepts. They involve examples that are created by applying the same unstated rule or transformation. The strategy for showing how single transformations work is to begin with examples that show minimum differences and then to move to examples that show larger differences. Let's look at an example of how this works. Look at Figure 7.

The juxtaposed examples at the beginning of these sequences show the learner just what changes in the examples cause changes in the responses. The test examples do not show this relationship but require the learner to apply the transformation demonstrated through the examples at the beginning of the sequence.

Bracket 1 indicates that all examples are created in basically the same way (verbal presentation by the teacher) and that the learner does the same thing with all juxtaposed examples (tells the answer). Bracket 2 shows minimum differences. Only one change in the preceding example creates the next example, and each change is relatively small.

Brackets 3 and 4 indicate that examples showing same-

Design Format

Figure 6

The sequence in Figure 6 introduces only one new discrimination—black oak.

Examples	Teacher Wording
	This is a black oak.
	This is a black oak.
	What is this?
	What is this?
	What is this?
	What is this?
	What is this?
	What is this?

Figure 7

Examples	Teacher Wording
	My turn.
1. 4 + 1 =	What is the answer? 5
2. 14 + 1 =	What is the answer? 15
3. 15 + 1 =	What is the answer? 16
4. 5 + 1 =	Your turn. What is the answer?
5. 6 + 1 =	What is the answer?
6. 9 + 1 =	What is the answer?
7. 5 + 1 =	What is the answer?
8. 1 + 1 =	What is the answer?
9. 16 + 1 =	What is the answer?
10. 8 + 1 =	What is the answer?
11. 3 + 1 =	What is the answer?
12. 12 + 1 =	What is the answer?

Design Format

nesses occur near the end of the sequence, after the learner has been shown how differences affect the responses.

By following the form above, we could teach an incredibly large variety of concepts.

Variations of the production-response sequence include elaborate ones that teach double transformations, such as the relationship between the percents: (five percent, 22.5 percent, or 3000 percent), and corresponding fractions: $\frac{5}{100}$ $\frac{22.5}{100}$ $\frac{3000}{100}$

Sentence-Relationship Discriminations

Not every discrimination involves a single word or fixed phrase. Some discriminations are expressed through sentences. In its simplest form, the sentence expresses a relationship between two discriminations that the learner can already label. Let's say the learner has already been taught the discrimination *moving faster* (through a choice-response sequence that shows the same object moving at different speeds and that requires the learner to label whether the object is *moving faster* or *not moving faster*). Let's say that we have also taught the discrimination *harder to stop* (using a choice-response sequence that presents examples of a moving thing and that requires the learner to indicate whether each example is harder to stop). We could now teach a unique sentence relationship that involves the label *faster* and the label *harder to stop: The faster it moves, the harder it is to stop.* Note that this relationship is something new. The analysis of the discrimination *moving faster* would not imply the relationship; nor would the analysis of *harder to stop.* Rather, the relationship is created by joining the two discriminations in a way that each retains its integrity. (In the sentence, "The faster it moves, the harder it is to stop," the *faster* and *harder to stop* refer to the same things they refer to in the initial teaching sequences. The sentence permits joining these labels in a way that creates a new discrimination or concept.)

To test whether a discrimination is a sentence relationship, ask the question, "Why?" or "How do you know?" The answer requires a full-sentence response and implies a sentence relationship that holds for a range of situations. A mother asks her child, "Why are you laughing?" The answer: "Jamey dropped his ice cream cone in the sink." The answer implies a sentence relationship: "If Jamey drops his ice cream cone in the sink, I laugh." This relationship is assumed to hold for a range of situations. If the same situation happened again (Jamey dropping the ice cream cone), the same response could be expected from the laughing child.

One more example: If we ask a friend, "Why aren't you going to Fran's party?," the response called for is a sentence, not a single word or phrase. The response must express a "rule" that holds in a variety of similar situations. Let's say that the respondent says: "Because I'm short of money." The implied sentence relationship: "If I'm short of money, I will not go to (Fran's) parties." According to this sentence relationship, we would expect the speaker to behave predictably in a variety of situations.

To teach sentence relationships, we must show the relationship between the two component discriminations that are joined in the relationship. To do this, *we use the same sequence of examples that would be used to teach the discrimination that occurs first in the sentence. However, for each example we ask a question about the discrimination that occurs last in the sentence.* Let's say that we wish to teach the relationship: the *wider* the stream, the *slower* it moves. The first mentioned discrimination is *wider,* so we would show a sequence of examples of *wider, not wider.* However, for each example, we would ask a question about *how slowly* the stream moves, not about wider. Figure 8 gives a possible sequence.

Figure 8

Teacher: We are going to talk about a stream that moves along without getting steeper. I will hold up my hands to show how wide the stream is.

Examples   **Teacher Wording**

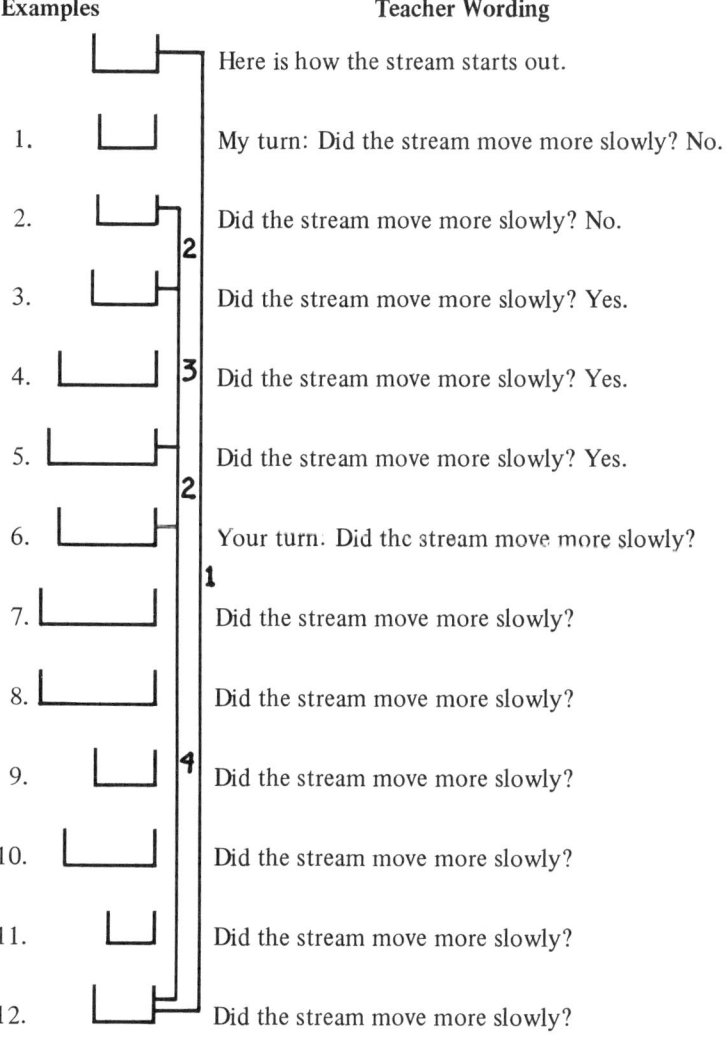

Here is how the stream starts out.

1. My turn: Did the stream move more slowly? No.
2. Did the stream move more slowly? No.
3. Did the stream move more slowly? Yes.
4. Did the stream move more slowly? Yes.
5. Did the stream move more slowly? Yes.
6. Your turn. Did the stream move more slowly?
7. Did the stream move more slowly?
8. Did the stream move more slowly?
9. Did the stream move more slowly?
10. Did the stream move more slowly?
11. Did the stream move more slowly?
12. Did the stream move more slowly?

The sequence of examples is the same that the teacher might present for teaching the discrimination *getting wider*. But the teacher doesn't ask about getting wider. The question asks about whether the stream moved more slowly. This sequence is capable of teaching the relationship between *wider* and *more slowly*, because the sequence shows that a change in width creates a corresponding change in speed. To assure communication of the desired interpretation, however, we must pre-teach the meaning of the component labels, *moving faster* and *getting wider*. If this pre-teaching is not done, the sequence above might teach the misrule that another label for "getting wider" is "moving more slowly."

If we wish the learner to provide us with evidence that he or she can express the relationship between getting wider and moving slower, we can present a variation of the sequence that involves *two questions* for each example, not one.

Here are two examples from that sequence.

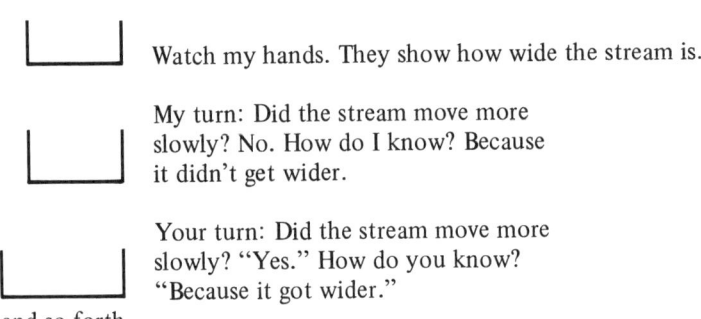

and so forth

This variation does not require the learner to repeat the entire rule, but merely to tell *what he or she observed in the example* that led to his or her judgment about whether the stream moved more slowly.

A final variation would make the rule explicit. Before the learner applied the rule to a sequence of examples, the learner would first say the rule and would apply it to purely verbal examples. Here is the first part of such a sequence.

Design Format 63

> Teacher: Here is the rule: When a stream gets wider, it moves slower. Say that rule.
> Stream R starts to get wider. So what else happens?
> A stream in the Rocky Mountains gets wider. So what else happens?

Following this activity would be the sequence of hard examples.

Note that even if the rule is stated and repeated, the sequence of examples should follow. This sequence provides a good test of the expressed relationship.

By following the form for the sequence above, we can teach virtually any sentence relationship. (If it can be expressed in a sentence, we can design a sequence to teach it.) For instance, we could design a sequence to teach the relationship: If the leaf is pinnately venated and has rounded lobes, it is a white oak leaf. We would show different leaves and ask the learner whether or not each is a white oak. We could present a second question, "How do you know?," with each example. This question would require the learner to relate his or her observations about the vein pattern and the lobes of the examples. (That leaf doesn't have pointed lobes.... that leaf is pinnately venated and has pointed lobes.) All relationships, including definitions, can be presented through variations of the sentence-relationship sequence.

Designing Complex Strategies

We have dealt with these facts:

1. There are only three types of discriminations or tasks that appear in any complex routine: choice-response, production-response, and sentence-relationship.

2. All discriminations of a particular type can be taught through a variation of the same sequence.

These facts imply that we can analyze any complex routine and identify the various discriminations that are necessary.

Once we identify them, we can specify how to teach them. If a complex routine contains a production-response discrimination, we would specify a production-response sequence to establish initial teaching of this discrimination.

The examples of Direct Instruction previously presented in the Operational Description chapter show complex strategies. One task in the word-reading strategy is "Sound it out." This discrimination is a production-response and would be taught through a production-response sequence. Another task in the word-reading routine is "Say it fast." This is another production-response concept. To teach, "Say it fast," we would say the word slowly and then instruct the learner to "Say it fast." We would construct the sequence of examples according to the form for production-response single-transformation concepts.

Some of the tasks in the equations routine are sentence relationships. For instance, the teacher presents the problem $\frac{2}{5} = \frac{\Box}{7}$ and asks, "Where do you work first in this problem?" The answer is "On the bottom." The reason is that the box is on the top. Here is the first part of a possible sequence for teaching this relationship.

$\frac{2}{5} = \frac{\Box}{7}$ Where do you work first?
             How do you know?

$\frac{2}{5} = \frac{7}{\Box}$ Where do you work first?
             How do you know?

$\frac{\Box}{2} = \frac{7}{5}$ Where do you work first?
             How do you know?

Diagnostic Teaching

With an understanding that complex activities are composed of the three discriminations, the teacher is in a good position to do diagnostic teaching. The procedure is simple.

Design Format

The teacher examines complex activities that are scheduled for the learner. A spelling activity may require the learners to identify "affixes" and consonants and CVC patterns. An arithmetic lesson may require the learner to identify the reciprocal of a fraction and to create fractions equal to one. The assumption of diagnostic teaching is that if each discrimination involved in these later activities is not taught and if these discriminations are possible causes of failure in the later activities, they must be pre-taught. For example, if the activity involving affixes, consonants, and CVC patterns is designed so that the learner might fail to perform if the learner doesn't have a good understanding of consonants, the discrimination of consonant, not-consonant must be pre-taught. Similarly, if the activity is designed so that the learner could fail if the learner isn't able to discriminate between an affix and word parts that are not affixes, the discrimination *affix* must be pre-taught.

This type of diagnostic teaching is preventative; a label that implies that the teacher provides the prescription before the learner is observed to have problems. Another type of diagnostic teaching is called reactive teaching. This type is initiated when the teacher discovers that the learner fails a complex activity because the learner is not firm on one or more of the component discriminations. The remedy is the same—teach the discrimination through the appropriate sequence. The only difference is that the discrimination is taught after a problem has been observed.

Whether the procedure is preventative or reactive, diagnostic teaching involves teaching discriminations that are components in complex activities. The discrimination is either a choice-response discrimination, a production-response discrimination, or a sentence-relationship discrimination and can be effectively taught through the appropriate sequence.

Formulating Complex Strategies

Although all complex routines are composed of the three types of discriminations, knowledge of these discriminations does not imply how to go about designing complex strategies, such as an operation for decoding regular words, a routine for identifying fallacies in arguments, or an attack on a particular class of equations. The most important point about these cognitive or symbolic operations is that they are generically different from "motor" operations, like throwing a ball, opening a door, eating with a fork, etc. Some theorists, particularly Piaget and his followers, encounter serious problems because they have not adequately analyzed the essential differences between cognitive and motor operations. For all motor operations, these statements are true:

1. All behavior that leads to the desired goal is *overt*.

2. The goal of the operation is reached only if all component behaviors are properly executed.

3. The operation has a built-in feedback system: If the goal is not reached, the learner is provided with information that some component behavior is inadequate. Conversely, if the goal is reached, the learner is provided with information that what the learner did is perfectly adequate.

This analysis suggests that the physical environment will provide a great deal of "teaching" of motor behaviors. Let's say that the learner is trying to throw a ball at a target, and that the learner understands the goal–hitting the target. According to Point 1 above, the learner cannot achieve the goal without producing overt responses. (The learner cannot throw the ball without moving his or her arm, without grasping the ball, without releasing the ball, etc.) What goes on in the learner's mind is perfectly irrelevant. According to Point 2 above, we can totally explain whether the learner achieves the goal by referring to the component behaviors—whether the learner fails to move his or her arm fast enough, let go of the ball at the appropriate time, etc. Note that the outcome is always fully explicable in terms of observed, overt behavior.

Design Format

Point 3 above indicates that the learner receives feedback on every trial. The learner will achieve the goal only if the overt behaviors are executed adequately. For each trial, the learner is *shown* whether the behaviors were properly executed. When the ball hits the target, the learner receives a message that what he or she did to reach a goal was perfectly adequate. If the ball misses the target, the learner is provided with information that he or she should change what he or she did. On every trial, the environment provides information about the appropriateness of the learner's behavior.

Cognitive behaviors are totally different from motor operations.

1. The behaviors that lead to the goal are not necessarily overt.
2. Reaching the goal, therefore, is not dependent upon a sequence of overt behaviors.
3. There is no feedback that is provided on each trial.

Consider word reading. You can read the word *mat* without making overt responses, although if you wish, you could read it out loud. If you read the word as "mash," however, you would receive precisely no feedback from the physical environment that your response is inappropriate. In fact, you could announce that the word is "elephant" and the physical environment would provide no feedback. If you tried hitting the target by sitting on the ball, you would be provided with immediate feedback that the behavior of sitting does not lead to hitting the target. If you tried opening a door without turning the door knob, you would be provided with immediate feedback that this behavior is inadequate. But if you read a word incorrectly, the physical environment has no provisions for responding to your attempt. Your goal was to read the word correctly, but the physical environment cannot let you know whether you reached this goal.

The Direct Instruction approach designs routines for

cognitive operations in a way that compensates for their inherent communication deficiencies. This is accomplished by:

(1) making all goal-related behaviors *overt*;
(2) designing these behaviors so that each plays a functional role in bringing the learner closer to the goal; and
(3) observing the overt behaviors of the learner as he or she applies the routine and is issued feedback about each trial.

By following these guidelines, we can judge when a routine is adequate. If the teacher can respond to each step the learner takes, and if each step is designed to bring the learner closer to the goal, the routine is adequate.

Note: These criteria for adequacy do not imply that the learner will perform without error. The reason for designing each step so that it is overt is that the teacher must be able to observe when the learner makes errors. If the routine has been designed so that the error can be immediately identified and corrected, the routine is adequate.

The word-reading routine in Figure 2 meets the criteria of efficiency.

1. The learner produces an overt response for each letter.
2. These responses are linked together in a way that leads to the pronunciation of the word. (The learner does not stop between the sounds. The learner then says the word faster.)
3. The teacher is in a position to provide feedback about whether the learner is producing appropriate responses.

If the learner has trouble with any of the component behaviors, a basic discrimination is implied. For instance, if the learner fails to say it fast after saying the word slowly, a production-response sequence is implied.

Design Format

Listen: mmmmmaaaa	Say it fast.
Mmmmmaaaannnnnnn	Say it fast.
mmmmmaaaaat	Say it fast.
sssssaaaat	Say it fast.
rrraaaat	Say it fast.
eeeeet	Say it fast.
etc.	

If the learner fails to identify one of the sounds correctly, a sound sequence is implied. Let us say the learner doesn't know the sound for *m*. The teacher presents the sounds: *m r a m s t m m t a m.* The teacher points to the first letter. The sound for this letter is *mmmm.* What sound? The teacher then says: "I'll point to each letter. You tell me the sound."

Structure and Responses

A complex routine is well-designed when *all instances of the routine are processed by following the same set of steps.* All instances of beginning word reading are processed through the same set of steps specified in the routine above. All instances of solving basic equations are processed through the same set of steps specified in the routine for equations (see Operational Description chapter). To appreciate the importance of this convention, think of a complex operation, such as working linear algebra problems, as discriminations that happen to be more involved than sentence-relationship discriminations. In one sense, these complex discriminations are like simple discriminations. If we respond to examples of simple discriminations in the same way, we show that these examples are the same in structure. So it is with complex discriminations. If we design the routine so that we respond to various examples in the same way, we show the learner that these examples have the same structure.

To convey this point to the learner, we must design the routine so that it is capable of processing a wide range of examples. The sequencing of these application examples follows the order of examples in a single-transformation sequence—examples that are similar occurring first, followed by juxtaposed examples that are dissimilar. If we process diverse examples through the same set of steps, we imply that these examples have the same structure and that their differences are irrelevant.

To illustrate this procedure, let us say that we design the routine in Figure 9 for teaching subtraction.

This routine meets the criteria of being overt, providing a sequence of behaviors that lead to the solution, and permitting the teacher to provide feedback on each step that is functional in reaching the solution.

The first examples of this operation would be similar to seven minus four. They might include 5-4, 7-2, 7-5, etc. (This set of examples corresponds to the first examples in the single-transformation sequence.) After the learner demonstrates understanding of these examples, however, the teacher would introduce a wide variety of examples, including negative number examples, as in the following illustration (see Figure 10).

The routine is nearly identical to that for solving positive number problems. By showing the learner that the same routine can be used for the full range of subtraction problems, we assure that the learner will learn that all these problems share the same structure. Without explaining this structure to the learner, we can teach this sophisticated discrimination.

The test of understanding, of course, is the learner's ability to solve problems other than those initially taught. If asked to make up different problems and solve them, children who are taught the subtraction operation above typically make up unique problems that may involve large numbers and that may lead to negative number answers.

The routine that is involved in the illustration above deals with a fairly elementary operation; however, we would

Figure 9

Teacher writes: 7 - 4 = ☐

Teacher: "Read it."

Learner reads problem.

Teacher: "Tell me what is on the side we work first."

Learner: "Seven minus four."

Teacher: "Tell me what to do first."

Learner: "Make seven lines under the seven."

Teacher does it: 7 - 4 = ☐
                   | | | | | | |

Teacher: "What do I do next?"

Learner: "Minus four."

Teacher crosses out four I's: 7 - 4 = ☐
                   | | | ɟɟɟɟ

Teacher: "How many are on the 7 - 4 side?"

Learner: "Three."

Teacher: "So tell me about the other side."

Learner: "There must be three on the other side."

Teacher writes "3" in the box: 7 - 4 = [3]
                   | | | ɟɟɟɟ

Figure 10

Teacher writes: 4 - 7 = ☐

Teacher: "Read it."

Teacher: "Tell me what is on the side we work first."

Learner: "Four minus seven."

Teacher: "Tell me what to do first."

Learner: "Make four lines under the four."

Teacher does it: 4 - 7 = ☐
                 ||||

Teacher: "What do I do next?"

Learner: "Minus seven."

Teacher makes seven horizontal lines: 4 - 7 = ☐
                                         ||||----

Teacher: "How many are on the 4 - 7 side?"

Learner: "Negative three."

Teacher: "So tell me about the other side."

Learner: "There must be negative three on the other side."

Teacher writes "-3" in the box: 4 - 7 = -3
                            ||||----

Design Format

follow the same design principles when dealing with more sophisticated cognitive operations. For instance, by using a routine that has the same set of steps, we could show the learner that ratio problems such as $\frac{4}{3} = \frac{9}{\Box}$ have the same essential structures as problems of the form: $4a = 9$
$3a = \Box$

Below, in Figure 11, are two problems with the routines for each.

Complex routines, such as the one above, are not borne from a few moments of thought. Nor do they come into existence in a fully-polished, final form. Typically, the final form is the last step in a series of approximations that is shaped by problems created when various examples and problems that different learners have in using the routine are presented. There is no tight formula for creating graceful routines except to retain a firm understanding of how completely efficient routines work. Then, just keep working toward this goal, using feedback received from learners—particularly those who have problems. They often provide you with the greatest information about how to make a complex routine slicker.

Motor Behavior

The sequences and routines that we have examined thus far are designed to teach cognitive skills or concepts, not to establish generically new responses. A generically new response is one the learner has never produced before and is incapable of producing, regardless of the reinforcement provided. Turning a summersault in the air and landing on one's feet is an example of a new response. Perhaps so is saying the sentence, "Sesquipedalianists exemplify pedantry." If the learner is incapable of producing the response when adequately motivated, the learner must learn the response. The difference between concept teaching and

Figure 11

$$\frac{4}{3} = \frac{9}{\square}$$

T: "Where do we work first?"

L: "On top."

T: "Which way do I draw the arrow?"

L: Points to the right.

T: Draws arrow: ⟶

T: "What does the problem on top say?"

L: "Four times some fraction equals nine."

T: "What fraction?"

L: "Nine-fourths."

T: Writes fraction: $\frac{4}{3} \xrightarrow{(\frac{9}{4})} \frac{9}{\square}$

T: "What do I do next?"

L: "Multiply by nine-fourths on the bottom."

T: Writes fraction on the bottom.

T: "What goes in the box?"

L: "Twenty-seven over four."

T: Writes answer:

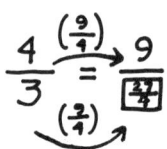

$$4a = 9$$
$$3a = \square$$

T: "Where do we work first?"

L: "On top."

T: "Which way do I draw the arrow?"

L: Points to the right.

T: Draws arrow: ⟶

T: "What does the problem on top say?"

L: "Four times some fraction equals nine."

T: "What fraction?"

L: "Nine-fourths."

T: Writes fraction: $4a \xrightarrow{(\frac{9}{4})} 9$ / $3a = \square$

T: "What do I do next?"

L: "Multiply by nine-fourths on the bottom."

T: Writes fraction on the bottom.

T: "What goes in the box?"

L: "Twenty-seven over four."

T: Writes answer:

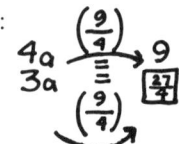

response teaching is that we can teach (or test) virtually any concept by using any response available—eye blink, hand movement, or answering *yes* or *no.* If the teaching demands new motor responses, we must teach the particular responses that are specified.

Perhaps the easiest way to think of motor responses is to think of the *body learning,* rather than the *mind learning.* Although we have some conscious control over new motor learning, it is not great. In fact, it is frequently an illusion. In learning to hit a curve ball, the batter can repeatedly tell himself or herself what he or she should do, and the batter will repeatedly miss the ball. Motor learning is slow. Furthermore, it doesn't follow the juxtaposition principles that apply to cognitive learning. The principles of juxtaposition are concerned with conveying information. New motor response teaching involves establishing new behavior, not conveying information. Massing examples *of a discrimination* helps provide necessary information—a map of the concept. Massing trials *of a new motor response* may produce rigid behavior and serious error patterns.

A complex routine may involve motor behavior—writing, manipulating, producing statements that are difficult to say, etc. Just as the discriminations should be pre-taught before the complex routine is introduced, the motor behaviors involved in a routine should be taught. The primary secret to their successful teaching is: provide adequate practice. Practice is deemed adequate when the learner can perform the newly taught response without assistance. There are mnemonics that can help organize the learner's approach to practice, but there is no substitute for practice.

Expanding What Is Taught

We have dealt with the *initial teaching* of concepts. The initial teaching is the most difficult to design, but it is certainly not sufficient to assure mastery. The initial teaching provides information about how the concept works and how it applies to a range of examples. This teaching, however, must be followed by application practice, if the concept is to be taught adequately.

During the initial teaching, the learner responds to the same question, such as, "Did it get wider?" The use of the same task for all examples reduces ambiguity in communicating with the learner; however, it does not show the learner the range of tasks that signal the concept *getting wider.* To remedy this deficiency, a variety of tasks should be introduced after the initial-teaching sequence is completed. These might include tasks in which the learner produces *manipulation responses* ("Make the space between those blocks wider."); tasks that involve *wh* questions ("Where is the wider stream... Which stream is the widest?..."); and other applications ("They wanted to build their fort where the river was the widest. Where is that?").

In addition to using different task forms, the expanded activities should *show a variety of new examples.* During the initial-teaching demonstration, the only objects shown for getting wider were hands. During the expansion, therefore, the learner should be shown that *wider* applies to many other contexts.

Expanding concepts is relatively easy if the designer follows the principle: What is taught is used. (The only reason for teaching something is that it is needed to clarify particular situations. Once the concept has been taught, therefore, the learner should be introduced to those situations that prompted the teaching.) The learner should not be taught a discrimination and then not see that discrimination for weeks or months. Once taught, the discrimination should be a nearly-daily part of the learner's instructional diet.

The fading or "unstructuring" of routines is part of the expansion process. Initially, the routine is "overtized," with every step designed so that the learner and teacher can observe it and respond to it. After the learner has mastered the basic routine, however, the learner should be guided in less structured applications. For instance, after the equations routine has been taught and practiced—in an overtized manner with a variety of problems—the learner should be required to work problems on his or her own and to apply the knowledge of ratios to hard problems that do not fall neatly into sentence packages.

Just as the instructional designer is responsible for teaching all component discriminations involved in a complex routine and for teaching the step-by-step execution of the routine, the designer is responsible for making the routine a covert property of the learner that is intuitive and natural. This transition will take place if the designer recognizes that this transition must be taught and that there must be adequate provisions for the learner to work problems on his or her own.

Summary

We have looked at the basic components of instruction, the teaching of basic discriminations, the design of complex cognitive routines, the teaching of motor responses, and the expansion of what is taught so that it proceeds from a highly controlled set of responses to an integral part of the learner's thinking process. We have devoted a disproportionate amount of effort on the basic discriminations, the building blocks of complex routines. Our treatment of motor responses and expansion discriminations is woefully inadequate; however, success in both these areas is probably more dependent upon adequate practice than clever instructional design. Certainly, careful design will make differences and will account for "savings" in the amount of time or the number of trials required by the learner. But without practice, the learning will not take place, and if the practice is not designed as well as it might be, the loss in learning rate is not great compared to the loss that occurs when cognitive discriminations are not initially taught well.

IV.

OUTCOMES

The typical outcome of Direct Instruction, if well-designed and adequately executed, is learning. A wide range of children learn, often far beyond expectations.

However, the greatest benefits may not be to children. Many competent people are engaged in teaching in the primary grades; however, only a small percentage teaches adequately. A larger percentage of intermediate and high school teachers is competent because knowledge of content becomes relatively more important than communication of content. With young children, students with a history of learning failure, and very naive learners, communication becomes extremely important.

The small percentage of adequate teachers has little to do with native ability or desire. The fact is that these teachers have probably never seen successful teaching. They may have seen people carry on discussions with the group, ask questions that are answered by the same handful of students, and provide seatwork and other work-by-yourself material that is supposed to provide "individualized" practice; however, they have never seen real demonstrable change in behavior that takes place rapidly and consistently when teaching is effective.

A Direct Instruction program is not a substitute for teacher training, but it works as a very good adjunct. Direct Instruction attempts to control every variable in the teaching environment that makes a difference in how the child performs. When the teacher works with high-performing children, control of these variables is relatively unimportant. When working with low performers, however, each detail becomes increasingly important—the pacing of the presentation, the clarity of the teacher's point, the use of signals, the type of correction, reinforcement, and repetition. We haven't discussed these details, but they have demonstrable effects on the attention and performance of the children. To repeat an earlier statement, unless all these variables are controlled with the very low performer, the entire effort often fails.

If the program has the potential for working, however, the teacher is in a much better position to learn about teaching behaviors and to receive a model of what successful teaching actually is.

Here is why:

1. The program provides the tasks and the script, which means that the teacher does not have to worry about designing these and about how these interface with one another (both during a given lesson and over long periods of time). The teacher can concentrate on executing the tasks—presenting and communicating skills to the children. After all, why should the teacher be required to be a curriculum designer? What training has been provided to assure even modest results in this enterprise? And when, precisely, is the teacher supposed to find time to analyze and develop a full-blown curriculum? A far more manageable endeavor would be to reduce the number of things the teacher is required to do and to concentrate on that which is central to the teaching role—*presenting*.

2. If the teacher presents well, the teacher will discover some facts about children, such as:

- Children are not unique. They appear unique only when one is not able to trace the learning of a concept or complex skill. If one observes the careful development of a skill—

Outcomes

beginning with the prerequisites and terminating with the unsupervised practice—one achieves a different perspective of children. They are reasonable. Granted, not all make the same mistakes, and granted some require more repetition than others; however, they are the same in a very important way. If the presentation is consistent with more than one interpretation, some children will fix on the wrong interpretation. Very rarely is a child's mistake "unique," "idiosyncratic," or "inexplicable" in terms of what the teacher did. For practical purposes, all mistakes committed by children are caused by the presentation. When the presentation is remedied, the mistakes diminish.

The confusion exhibited by the typical corrective reader in grade five is not only explicable in terms of what he or she has been taught, it is inexplicable in any other terms. The child reads in synonyms, calling *happy* "glad" and *a* "the." By what kind of neurological circuitry is this type of mistake possible? The answer lies not in the child's head but in what has been taught. Go back and look at the terrible misrules that were presented to this child. Listen to the first-grade teacher as he or she first talks about a picture and then reads the words under the picture. This routine is repeated—picture followed by words about the picture. This presentation is consistent with the interpretation that one reads words by first determining the *meaning*. This idea is further reinforced by the second-grade teacher who tries to help out the hapless child by encouraging him or her to "guess" about "what the word in that sentence *could* be." Again, the idea is reinforced that if you know the meaning, you can read the word. The children ultimately end up with a label—*dyslexia* or whatever; however, these children are the victims of twin sins, poor teaching and displaced labeling. Simply because they have the reading deficiency doesn't imply that they are the cause of the deficiency.

- Since children are not unique, since they make very

predictable mistakes, and since these mistakes are the fault of the presentation, it is generally not efficient to work one-on-one with children. The typical resource-teaching scene is a travesty of teaching, with the resource teacher engaging first in this and then in that, hoping (without much logical basis) that something will work and knowing that it is probably better to flit around in this manner than it is to stick with one thing and fail repeatedly. With a good program, it is far more effective to work with a group than it is with individuals. Motivating children is easier, and corrections are more economical.

• The teacher learns how children learn. Typically teachers have vague ideas of how many repetitions are required for an average learner to remember the sound for the symbol *r* or to remember to capitalize the first letter of a sentence. Much teacher irritation stems from lack of knowledge. The teacher supposes that the learner should perform after one trial, or perhaps after four. In fact, however, the child may require 30 trials. If the teacher does not discover this fact, the teacher ultimately will draw sour conclusions about children. Perhaps children are slow, indifferent, or handicapped. In any case, they don't learn in the same manner the teacher teaches. Direct Instruction provides the teacher with intense process information about the children, what they are doing, and how they are learning. The tasks are usually designed so that they are fairly simple, permitting the teacher to observe what it takes to induce new concepts and new skills.

3. In addition to learning about children, the teacher learns about instruction. One of the first things the teacher comes to appreciate is a poor task. We see this phenomenon in field tryouts of new Direct Instruction programs. Typically, we provide the minimum necessary training or orientation before the teachers receive the program. The reason is that we want to find out which aspects of training are needed most. The programs in their tryout form have rough spots,

but not everything in them is rough. The programs have been developed through extensions of the principles outlined in this book, and most of the tasks and sequences are quite workable, which means that the students respond to these activities in predictable ways. The rough spots, however, persist. Quite commonly, a tryout teacher who has never been involved in Direct Instruction before can identify these tasks and provide feedback about them. The difference between successful tasks and poor ones becomes quite obvious to these teachers *after they have worked with successful tasks.* The problem is that much instructional material contains no tasks that have the potential for being successful. They are too wordy; they try to teach far too much; or they do not exercise careful control of vocabulary. Often, the number of examples of a concept is a small fraction of what would be required to assure successful learner performance. A teacher who works with these programs is in a very poor position to identify poor tasks, because even those that are relatively successful are generally weak.

V.
DEVELOPMENTAL GUIDE

The purpose of this chapter is to provide basic guidelines and suggestions on how to develop Direct Instruction. This information is provided with the understanding that much of development is embedded in the design format already described. This chapter will, nonetheless, summarize the key developmental steps; i.e., elaborate upon where it is most efficient to develop Direct Instruction within an already busy schedule of ongoing developmental and implementation activity.

Developmental Hierarchies

As a part of development, we should look at the pitfalls that lie at either extreme of instructional design. At one extreme is what we might call the hierarchical approach to instructional design. Teachers and instructional designers who use this approach try to discover and analyze hierarchies of skills, with the idea that the hierarchy is somehow related to *developmental* principles. The grand design is supposed to be a sequence of skills that corresponds to the natural order of the growth pattern of the human. People who become engaged in this effort typically become facile at quoting what others say but poor at designing instruction. The reason is that objectives for any instructional program do not and cannot derive from developmental data, which tell only what children typically do, not what they *can* do. Furthermore, the classification systems are typically useless. They attempt to be exhaustive, but they are contrived. The general idea behind this approach is worthwhile—designing an overall interrelated sequence of instructional events; however, the emphasis is misplaced. The exhaustive classification system for the instructional design has to do with discriminations, which divide into three classes and which can be taught by following the form for a particular class.

Behavioral Objectives—Use and Misuse

At the other end of the spectrum is the atomic approach represented by the behavioral objective. Behavioral objectives are important, but too often they are misinterpreted. For example, an objective may state, "The child will orally read CVC words." This objective is like a two-edged sword. If it is used as a simple checklist of things to be taught, it is valuable. Certainly, the CVC word is one type that should be taught to the beginning reader, along with VCC, VC, CCVC, and others. The objective doesn't tell: (a) about other types of words that the learner will read, or (b) about other responses that the learner will produce with CVC words. The objective, in other words, does not tell us how to orchestrate the objective about reading CVC words with other activities. As a result, a teacher may design a sequence that achieves the stated objective but that does so at the expense of other objectives. If the naive learner reads only CVC words, the learner will later have trouble with VC words or VCC words. The reason is that the set of examples used to achieve the initial objective is consistent with the interpretation that reading involves *only* CVC words. The reader, after all, read no words that are not CVC words. To assure that the objective of reading CVC words is properly framed:

    1. We must make sure that the learner reads CVC words silently as well as orally and that the learner produces

Developmental Guide

other responses with these words. (If the learner always reads orally in the presence of CVC words, the presentation stipulates that this response is the only one possible.)

2. We must make sure that the learner reads word types other than CVC.

To achieve what began as a simple behavioral objective, we are now involved in a program that coordinates different responses and different types of examples. Furthermore, unless we become involved in a program, we will most certainly provide poor teaching. The learner may read quite proficiently when all the words on the page are short-*o* words; however, the fact that the learner performs in this situation does not provide evidence that he or she can read short-*o* words when the context includes not only other short-*o* words, but short-*a*, short-*u*, and short-*e* words. The problem is real. Earlier, we noted that some "easy" irregular words like *is* are introduced very early in DISTAR reading. The reason is that unless the children are shown early that there are irregulars (which is what happened in the early, prepublication tryout editions of the program), they have trouble with the idea that some words are irregular. Their response is natural. All the words they read were regular. Why shouldn't they suppose that *every* word is regular?

The point is that designing sequences or activities that achieve particular objectives should not be considered in a vacuum. Everything that is taught should be viewed in terms of related skills—both concurrent and future. If the articulation between these skills is not well-designed, each objective that is reached paralyzes other objectives.

Fixing Up Existing Programs

Instead of searching for elusive hierarchies of skill development, or trying to deal with isolated behavioral objectives, you are much better off fixing up existing programs, even though these may be quite faulty. They at least provide a "hierarchy" of skill progression and, therefore, a basic framework for coordinating different objectives. If you begin by accepting a program as a starting point, you will be able to add pieces to it to assure that it works, which means that all parts of it work, not merely a few isolated behavioral objectives.

Another advantage of working from existing programs and establishing your primary objective as a successful performance within this program is that the program relieves you of a great many instructional design decisions. The complex activities and applications toward which the program moves have already been designed. These complex activities are composed of basic discriminations. The program therefore provides information about which discriminations are needed and the precise ways that each is expressed. With this information, you can make up initial-teaching sequences for every discrimination that is not adequately taught.

Illustration. Let us say a program is trying to teach the concept of *noun* to third graders. The textbook defines a noun as, "A name-word is a noun." Perhaps two or three examples follow, but these do not show the difference between nouns and other words in the sentence. The teacher could use a production-response sequence to teach the discrimination. For example:

Examples
Dogs played.
Five dogs played.
Five cats played.
Five cats and dogs played.
Five dogs played with cats.
Five dogs played on a rug.
That rug was a dirty thing.
That rug was dirty.
My room was dirty.
That dirty rug was in my room.

Teacher Wording
My turn to name any nouns: Dogs
My turn to name any nouns: Dogs
Your turn. Name any nouns. Cats
Name any nouns. Cats, dogs
Name any nouns. Dogs, cats
Name any nouns. Dogs, rug
Name any nouns. Rug, thing
Name any nouns. Rug
Name any nouns. Room
Name any nouns. Rug, room

A clean mouse is in my room.	Name any nouns. Mouse, room
That mouse is nice.	Name any nouns. Mouse
That mouse is a nice animal.	Name any nouns. Mouse, animal

This sequence shows that nouns may occur in the subject or predicate of the sentence; however, this sequence does not teach all about nouns. Specifically, it doesn't show the difference between nouns and pronouns. When the topic of pronouns comes up, however, the teacher is in a good position to show what they are by contrasting them with nouns and presenting them in a choice-response sequence.

Often, textbook explanations present rules, principles, or explanations without teaching component words or sentence relationships that are expounded. Science, social studies, and arithmetic texts typically bury important principles in short explanations that are followed by peripheral applications. For example, a fifth-grade science text observes: "Newton's principle is the third law of motion. This law states that for every action, there is an equal and opposite reaction." Following this assertion is the application of the principle to a jet engine. The unfortunate implication is that the principle may be limited to jet engines. To teach this principle, the teacher could use a sentence-relationship sequence. The teacher would first state the rule, then establish how it works.

The teacher presents a picture of a boat. "I will show you which way the man jumps from the boat. That is the action. You show me which way the boat will move. That is the reaction."

Examples	Teacher Wording
	My turn. Show the reaction of the boat. Teacher points: How do you know the boat moved that way? Because the man moved in the opposite direction.

Your turn. Show the reaction of the boat...
How do you know the boat moved that way?

Show the reaction of the boat...
How do you know the boat moved that way?

Show the reaction of the boat...
How do you know the boat moved that way?

Show the reaction of the boat...
How do you know the boat moved that way?

After the learner has completed this sequence, an explanation of jet engines follows quite easily. The teacher shows which way the burning gases move. The learner shows the direction of the reaction. The teacher points out that the engine is attached to the wing, which means that if the engine moves forward, the wing moves forward, too. The learner is now provided with an adequate explanation of why the plane moves forward. More important, however, the learner is taught action and reaction as a principle, not as an idiom that applies merely to jet engines.

Procedures

To fix up existing programs, follow these steps:
1. Analyze the program by looking at the later complex activities that are scheduled for the learner; note the component discriminations that occur in these.
2. Back up in the program and see how each is taught.
3. Identify whether the teaching for each component discrimination is adequate (which means that it is consistent with one and only one interpretation).
4. If not, design initial-teaching presentations (possibly only for those discriminations that are most critical for later tasks).
5. If possible, design the initial-teaching sequences so each uses the same wording that is called for in the complex activities.

Developmental Guide

6. Schedule these initial-teaching sequences so that the learner masters them before encountering the complex activities.
7. Try out the revised program with naive learners and *respond to the feedback.*

All the points above are important, but perhaps Point 7 is most important. You will make mistakes in designing sequences that teach cognitive skills. But if you present the material in a carefully controlled manner to naive learners, they will show you, through their responses, just where your sequences are lumpy. If you design some sequences well, their performance on these sequences becomes your baseline. The way they respond to these sequences is the way they should respond to all. If they don't, there are problems with the sequence. Most probably, the wording is awkward or the sequence does not permit rapid enough presentation of the examples. Change it.

Once you have fixed up a program, you may discover that the program does not achieve some of the goals that you have for the learners. You are now in a good position to either add these to the program or to discard the program in favor of another. But at this point, you have a great deal of knowledge of how to achieve the learning for a given set of complex skills and how the component discriminations may be coordinated in a way that permits the learner to reach many related behavioral objectives.

Firming the Learner

Our discussion of initial-teaching sequences may have suggested that learning takes place after the learner is exposed to one sequence. In many cases, it does. Usually, however, the learner's memory for the new discrimination will decay, and the new discriminations must be firmed through initial-teaching sequences on at least two consecutive lessons. When a second initial-teaching sequence is presented, it should differ from the first. Possibly, the common set of features for all the examples in the sequence is different. Certainly, the order of the items is different.

When constructing sequences, follow the guide of designing the first part of the sequence so that it shows how the discrimination works. (Follow the principles of juxtaposition for showing differences and samenesses. Then test through a series of examples.)

While going through a sequence, the learner may make mistakes. If the sequence is well-designed, the learner can be firmed or corrected by following these three steps:

1. Model the correct answer to the item missed.
2. Test the learner on this item.
3. Back up two items in the sequence and test on all items in order.

This correction reduces the learner's tendency to make the same mistake again. The reason is that the sequence very carefully controls the difficulty of each item. In the earlier parts of the sequence, an item is juxtaposed to items that differ in few ways. In later parts of the sequence, juxtaposed items differ in many ways, implying that the context for each item is less prompted by the previous items. If the learner makes a mistake early in the sequence, his or her mistake indicates that he or she has trouble with the item when it appears in a very simple, highly prompted context. The correction is achieved by modeling the correct answer, testing on the item missed, backing up two items, and testing on all the items in sequence. When the missed item is repeated as part of this sequence, it appears once more in a highly prompted context.

If the learner makes a mistake later in the sequence, his or her response indicates that he or she has trouble with the item when it appears in an unprompted context. An appropriate correction does *not* involve returning to an earlier part of the sequence and repeating these tasks, because the learner can perform well on items in the juxtaposition context of the early part of the sequence. What the learner needs is practice on the item in the less-prompted context. This remedy is achieved simply by modeling the correct answer, testing on the item missed, backing up two items, and testing on all the items in sequence. When the missed item is repeated as the final part of this correction procedure, it occurs within the context that gives the learner problems.

If the learner makes a relatively high percentage of errors on the test items in a sequence (erring on 25 percent or more of these items), follow this procedure:
1. Use the standard correction procedure outlined above to firm the learner on each error.
2. Follow the sequence with a parallel sequence that deals with the same discrimination but that presents different items and a different pattern of juxtaposition (possibly a shorter sequence).

A similar remedy is called for if the learner makes mistakes when going through a complex activity. Perhaps a discrimination in the complex activity had not been pre-taught (because the instructional designer thought that the learners probably knew it), and the learner shows through his or her responses that he or she does not know the discrimination. Although you may not be able to provide this remedy immediately, it should involve a sequence that provides initial teaching of the discrimination, followed by the complex activity that involves the discrimination. The teaching of this discrimination would, of course, become part of the revised program.

Firming Motor Responses

Not everything that you will teach involves cognitive discriminations. New motor responses must be taught. Unlike the awareness of discriminations, these skills must be shaped—molded gradually—through repeated practice. The strategy for achieving new motor responses (saying poems,

writing at a specified rate, solving arithmetic problems at a specified rate) involves changing the criterion that leads to some form of reinforcement. Here are the general guidelines:
1. Use the learner's initial performance (number correct or rate) as a baseline.
2. Set the initial criterion of performance so that if the learner performs at baseline, he or she would receive either reinforcement on 75 percent of the trials or 75 percent of the total possible reinforcement.
3. When the learner's performance improves to the point that the learner receives reinforcement on either 85 percent of the trials or 85 percent of the total possible reinforcement, change the criterion so that it again becomes 75-75 percent.
4. Continue until the learner has learned the motor skill acceptably.

Summary

How can you use Direct Instruction?

To fix up existing program sequences. The hallmark of an adequate sequence is that the learner is taught all discriminations needed for complex activities. Conversely, complex activities cannot be failed because some of the component discriminations have not been taught.

To fix up a program, you begin with complex applications presented in the program, identify discriminations that have not been taught, design sequences appropriate for the teaching of each discrimination, and schedule these sequences as they occur before the learner is required to engage in the complex application. This approach permits you to deal with a hierarchy of skills (building blocks that lead to a complex structure) and to specify behavioral objectives (the various discriminations and skills implied by the complex applications).

An essential part of any program fix-up is tryout information. The specific problems that learners encounter when going through the revised sequence signal additional teaching that is needed.

Not everything that you will teach is a basic discrimination. Motor response teaching requires time and practice. The teaching should be designed so that the learner's performance serves as a guide as to how fast to "shape" responses, and the teaching should use reinforcement. Reinforcement provides the learner with a "reason" for improving.

VI.

RESOURCES

This chapter provides a list of Direct Instruction programs with indications of how each might be helpful in illustrating points made in this book. When you examine these programs, you may observe that the sequences used to teach discriminations often take a form different from that specified in this book. Understand that the sequences used in the commercial programs are not superior to the ones created by following the principles outlined in this book. The material designed for commercial programs is simply more manageable for the printed-page format. Illustrations are often used to supplant continuous conversion of examples. Illustrations actually do not work as well because they require the learner to extract information from a comparison of static examples (instead of being shown which changes occur to convert one example into the next). Illustrations, however, are more practical and take better advantage of the printed page.

Another difference you may observe is that sequences of examples are shorter in the commercial programs and that they are distributed over a few days. (Initial teaching of any skill typically occurs on three or more consecutive lessons.) This conversion is not superior but practical. It would probably be possible to design the presentation so that the teacher presents it one time, on one lesson, followed by expansion activities. However, two things may go wrong with this formula. The teacher may present it poorly, and some children may be absent. By repeating a variation of the presentation on three or more lessons, we increase the possibility that the teacher will present it adequately. We also automatically compensate for routine absences.

Other details of these programs derive from considerations of time, energy, and manageability; however, if you follow the development of a discrimination or a complex skill, you will discover that it follows the same basic principles outlined in this book, and it attempts to achieve the goal of presentations that work for the full range of possible examples and that are consistent with one and only one interpretation.

MATERIAL

Engelmann, S., and Osborn, J. *DISTAR Language* 1 and 2. Chicago: SRA.

The revised editions of the language program provide many discrimination examples. One of the more valuable "tracks" or developmental sequences of activities in the program is the action track. First, actions are taught; then they are chained together in a review series. The programs also provide good examples of how to integrate skills into problem-solving activities. These are called "concept applications." After children have learned prepositions, concept application tasks involving prepositions would appear. This application might also require the learner to use other skills that have been taught.

Engelmann, S., and Osborn, J. *DISTAR Language* 3. Chicago: SRA.

This program has a more limited scope than that of *DISTAR Language* 1 and 2. *Language* 3 is primarily a grammar program, dealing with subject-predicate, sentence, and various sentence types. Students do not have to go through *Language* 1 and 2 to begin 3. The program provides examples of sequences that teach discriminations, such as whether a sentence is a statement, question, or command.

Engelmann, S., and Carnine, D. *DISTAR Arithmetic* 1 and 2. Chicago: SRA.

The revised programs provide good examples of teaching basic discriminations and then embedding them into more complex operations. *Arithmetic* 1 teaches the basic operations of addition, algebra addition, and subtraction. Multiplication is introduced in *Arithmetic* 2. The pre-teaching of operations begins with counting and with application of the equality rule: You must end up with the same number on this side as on the other side. Every operation is shown to be a different type of counting operation, controlled by the sign in the problem. The problem-solving game that is played with every problem is governed by the equality rule (make the sides so that both have the same number).

Engelmann, S., and Carnine, D. *DISTAR Arithmetic* 3. Chicago: SRA.

I don't recommend using this program as a follow-up to *Arithmetic* 2. Although it contains sound presentations and skill emphasis, it has not been revised to articulate well with *Arithmetic* 2. Hopefully, it will be revised soon.

Engelmann, S., and Bruner, E. *DISTAR Reading* 1 and 2. Chicago: SRA.

If you work with average performing Kindergarten or first graders, do not use *DISTAR Reading* 1. Instead, order the *DISTAR Fast Cycle* program or use *Reading* 2, which contains the *Fast Cycle* program. The *Fast Cycle* program contains 70 lessons and teaches the same skills that are taught in the 160 lessons of *Reading* 1. By the end of *Reading* 2, the children are handling fairly sophisticated comprehension activities. A series of stories at the end of *Reading* 2 involves a girl who dreams she is in a strange land. To leave the land, she must learn 16 rules. The stories are written in a way that requires the children to remember and to apply the rules.

Engelmann, S., and Stearns, S. *DISTAR Reading* 3. Chicago: SRA.

This program teaches children how to read for new information; how to permit the printed page to teach. It establishes the kind of rehearsal behavior needed to retain and apply information. So far as I know, it is the only reading program that actually teaches how to read for information. Children may be placed in *Reading* 3, if they decode adequately. They do not have to go through *DISTAR Reading* 1 and 2 to be placed in *Reading* 3.

    Engelmann, S., Carnine, L., and Johnson, G. *Corrective Reading,* Decoding A. Chicago: SRA.

This program teaches basic decoding to the older-corrective reader who has very limited reading ability. The program differs from DISTAR reading in that it does not use special type faces or other orthographic conventions. A strong word pronunciation track goes through the entire 60-lesson program.

    Engelmann, S., Johnson, G., Becker, W., Meyers, L., Carnine, L., and Becker, J. *Corrective Reading,* Decoding B. Chicago: SRA.

This program involves daily word-attack exercises and story reading. The program teaches a consistent word-reading strategy, which is what the typical corrective reader lacks. Unlike a "teaching" program, this program provides the enormous amount of repetition required to re-teach the learner. Specific attack skills are taught through cycles that present the skill first in the simplest context (a series of continuous conversion examples) and then in more difficult contexts. The final and most difficult context in the cycle is that of connected sentences. Here, the learner has practiced a variety of abortive strategies for decoding. Here, the old habits persist. Most poor readers in grades 4-12 place in Decoding B, starting at either Lesson 1 or 61.

    Engelmann, S., Meyers, L., Johnson, G., and Carnine, L. *Corrective Reading,* Decoding C. Chicago: SRA.

This program extends the skills taught in Decoding B. More

sophisticated vocabulary and sentence structures are taught. Decoding C introduces the reading of expository material as well as stories. Also, beginning with Lesson 71, a part of most lessons involves reading a passage selected from a magazine or newspaper. The same procedure used to attack passages from the Decoding C student book is applied to outside material.

Engelmann, S., Haddox, P., Hanner, S., and Osborn, J. *Corrective Reading,* Comprehension A. Chicago: SRA.

This program stresses three types of skills, each of which is presented on every lesson: thinking operations, worksheet activities, and information. The thinking operations include work on classification, deductions, analogies, true-false, and definitions. Worksheet activities reinforce each of the thinking operations skills. The program provides many good examples of sequences for teaching various discriminations. The program also provides good examples of routines that teach the student to analyze analogies and to attend to details of descriptions.

Engelmann, S., Osborn, S., and Hanner, S. *Corrective Reading,* Comprehension B. Chicago: SRA.

This program embraces an extraordinary amount of integrated teaching. All tracks teach skills and new information. What is taught in one track is then used in all other tracks. The program focuses on reasoning skills (deductions, the use of basic evidence identifying contradictions), information skills (nomenclature of body systems, such as the respiratory system, and rules that govern these systems), sentence skills (combining sentences, analyzing them), following directions, and writing skills (including editing). The program teaches an enormous amount. The development of skills such as deductions is particularly interesting. Because this program teaches skills that are not taught in development reading comprehension programs, it is used increasingly with "regular" classroom students, particularly in grades six through eight.

Dixon, R. *Morphographic Spelling.* Eugene: E-B Press.
This program is probably the least offensive to the teacher who has never engaged in Direct Instruction. The reason is that teachers generally appreciate the fact that you must spell words out loud to learn how to spell them and that this overt spelling is a reasonable activity. The program presents variations of a few basic spelling rules—beginning with the rules that all words are made up of morphographs and a morphograph is the smallest unit of meaning in the word. The rules for joining morphographs (re-, -ing, dis-, to base words and non-word bases) are explained in terms of the way each morphograph is spelled. The program provides many examples of how sentence relationships are expressed as rules and are applied to various examples.

All Direct Instruction programs are accompanied by teachers' guides that provide information about the development of the various skills, show the routines or formats for teaching the skills, and provide information about more common mistakes and how to correct them. These guides provide rationale for the development of the overall approach. In addition to the guides for the individual corrective reading programs, there is a series guide and a manual, *Implementing the Corrective Reading Series* (published by E-B Press). This manual tells how to set up the program if it is to be used in various classrooms of a school district. It provides valuable information about placement and evaluation.

Becker, W., Engelmann, S., and Thomas, D. Teaching 1: *Classroom Management*

Becker, W., Engelmann, S., and Thomas, D. Teaching 2: *Cognitive Learning and Instruction*

Becker, W., and Engelmann, S. Teaching 3: *Evaluation of Instruction*

These books, published by SRA, relate Direct Instruction to principles of operant psychology and to traditional methods

Resources *103*

of evaluating instructional outcomes. They are useful for identifying how and why Direct Instruction is different from other approaches. The reasons are based either on facts about the way children learn or on some form of logical analysis.

VII.

APPENDIX

The facts and principles presented in this book have been investigated by Carnine (1978). Below is a list of important facts and principles as well as brief summaries of studies that investigated each fact and principle.

Facts

Fact: *The presence of the same features in both positive and negative examples rules out possible interpretations.* Carnine investigated this fact by assigning 38 college students to one of three treatments. The same artificial concept was presented in all three treatments. Geometric figures with one, two, or three points were treated as positive examples, and examples with four or five points were treated as negative examples. In one treatment, a dot pattern appeared in both positive and negative examples. Since this feature appeared in both positive and negative examples, the dot pattern could not be a basis for determining whether the example was positive or negative. In a second treatment, the dots appeared *only* in positive examples (figures with one, two, or three points). In the third treatment, the dots appeared *only* in negative examples (figures with four or five points). When dots appeared in both positive and negative examples, subjects responded correctly to transfer items on almost 100 percent of the trials. Subjects receiving the positive-and-negative examples responded to the number of points. When dots appeared only in positive examples, almost 100 percent of the subjects responded to the presence of dots (failing about 50 percent of the transfer items). Similarly, almost all subjects in the third treatment group (dots present only in negative examples) responded to the absence of dots on a transfer test (treating items as negatives only if they had dots).

Features that appear in both positives and negatives cannot be a basis for an example being either positive or negative. The presence of dots in both positives and negatives provides the learner with information about the dots: they are not relevant. One reason the continuous-conversion sequences are effective is that the same irrelevant features appear in all examples—positive and negative. The sequence, therefore, demonstrates that these features are irrelevant to the discrimination.

Fact: *A negative example rules out the maximum number of interpretations when the negative example is least different from some positive example.* Carnine developed five sets of examples. All had the same positives but different negatives (see Figure 12). Set *A* shows the minimum difference between positive and negative, while Set *E* contains no negative and therefore generates a large number of possible interpretations.

Carnine presented a different set of examples to five different groups of preschoolers (four-six years). There were 13 children in each group. After receiving a fixed number of demonstration examples, each child received a transfer test. Children presented with Set *A* examples responded correctly to 10.2 transfer items, while children presented with Set *E* responded correctly to only 5.0 transfer items. The trend clearly suggests that the greater the number of *possible* interpretations, the greater the probability that some students will learn an interpretation other than the one intended

Appendix 107

Figure 12

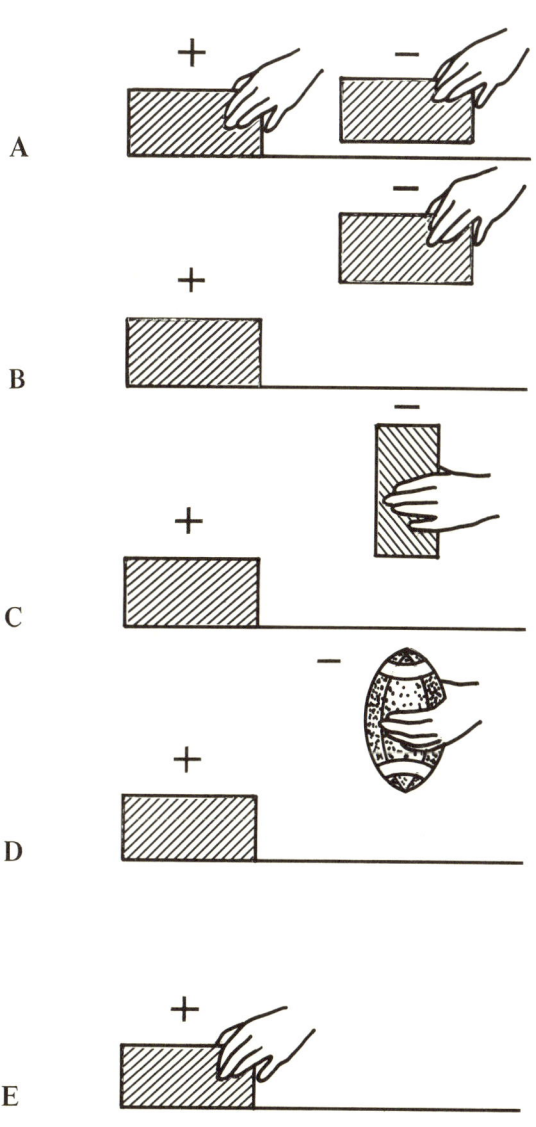

by the teacher. The trend also confirms that the greater the difference between positives and negatives, the greater the number of interpretations.

Fact: *Continuous conversions increase the obviousness of the difference between positive and negative examples.* Carnine compared continuous- and non-continuous-conversion sequences in two different studies. In the first study, 40 preschoolers were randomly assigned to a continuous or non-continuous presentation of the concept *diagonal.* In the second study, 40 different preschoolers were randomly assigned to continuous or non-continuous presentations of *convex.* In the continuous-conversion treatment for *diagonal,* a line segment was rotated to generate positive and negative examples. For continuous conversion of *convex,* a wire was moved to create positive and negative examples of *convex* or *not-convex.* In both studies, the same set of positive and negative examples was also presented non-continuously.

For both studies, the continuous-conversion groups met the criterion of performance (mastered the concepts) in significantly fewer trials.

Principles

Principle 1: *The correct interpretation is communicated most efficiently if the same "setup" features appear in all examples.* The maximum number of shared setup features is achieved if all examples are created through continuous conversion. (The continuous creation of examples assures that the example is changed to the minimum amount needed to create another example.) Tennyson, Woolley, and Merrill (1972) have suggested that an efficient procedure is one that changes the setup features every third example. (Two examples with the same setup features are presented, followed by two examples with new setup features.)

To challenge this conclusion, Carnine taught the discrimination of *90° or more* using three different variations in the

Appendix

setup features. For the continuous-conversion group, all examples were created through continuous conversion. For the non-continuous-conversion group, the same set of examples and the same order of examples were used. The examples, however, were shown on cards and were not created through continuous conversion. For the paired setup group, the same setup features appeared in two juxtaposed examples and were replaced by different setup features in the next pair of examples.

All students then received training on the same set of "transfer" examples. These examples were non-continuous and contained setup features that were found in none of the earlier training examples. A student completed the training after meeting a specified criterion of performance on the transfer items.

The most efficient procedure proved to be the continuous-conversion presentation. The mean trials to criterion for students in this group was 10.6. The non-continuous procedure was the next most efficient (with mean trials to criterion of 15.8). The least efficient procedure was the paired setup presentation. Students required an average of 26.0 trials to meet the specified criterion of performance.

Principle 2: *When minimum-difference examples are juxtaposed, the intended interpretation is made most obvious.* Granzin and Carnine (1977) conducted three studies that compared the effects of minimum-difference juxtapositions of positive and negative examples. In the first study, 44 first graders were randomly assigned to one of two treatment groups. Both groups received the same set of positive and negative examples. The only difference was the juxtapositions of the examples. Minimally different positive and negative examples were juxtaposed in one treatment; maximally different examples were juxtaposed in the other treatment.

The number of training trials needed for students to reach

a specified criterion of performance was significantly lower for the minimum-difference juxtaposition group. This group required 17.4 trials to meet criterion. The students in the maximum-difference juxtaposition group required 29.9 trials to meet criterion.

A second study investigated whether the advantage of the minimum-difference juxtaposition pattern held when first-grade children were taught a conjunctive concept (examples being positive only if more than one feature is present). A third study presented second graders with a disjunctive concept (examples being positive, if one of a set of possible features is present) and with a different conjunctive concept. The pattern of performance was the same for all studies. Children who received the minimum-difference juxtaposition treatment reached the training criterion for the conjunctive concept in 8.1 trials, while the children in maximum-difference juxtaposition treatment required 19.1 trials. For the disjunctive concept, the minimum-difference children required 21.1 trials, while the maximum-difference children required 37.1 trials.

Principle 3: *Juxtaposed examples that differ greatly show the sameness among positives.* In a study conducted by Carnine, one group of children was shown a wider variation of positive examples than another group.

Forty-seven students in grades one to five, who had some knowledge of fractions but no knowledge of decimals, were randomly assigned to the groups. Both groups received the same number of demonstrations about how to convert fractions with denominators of 100 into their decimal equivalents. The Full Range group received demonstrations with three types of fraction-to-decimal conversions (X/100 to .0X; XX/100 to .XX; XXX/100 to X.XX). The Restricted Range group received demonstrations of only one type of conversion (XX/100 to .XX). Children in the Restricted Range group converted significantly fewer fractions to

Appendix

decimals on a transfer test, which presented new examples of all three types of fractions.

The Full Range group successfully performed on 28 transfer items, whereas the Restricted Range group performed on only 12.3 transfer items.

Carnine has conducted other studies that document the use of other details of Direct Instruction—uniform, scripted wording; relatively fast pacing; high response rate; etc. These studies show a correspondence between what would be predicted logically, on the basis of analysis of communication between teacher and learner, and what is found experimentally.

References

Carnine, D.W. *Formative Research Studies on Direct Instruction.* Follow Through Project, Appendix A to Technical Report #78-1. Unpublished manuscript, University of Oregon, Eugene, Oregon, 1978.

Granzin, A.C., and Carnine, D.W. Child Performance on Discrimination Tasks: Effects of Amount of Stimulus Variation. *Journal of Educational Psychology,* 1977, *67,* 909-912.

Tennyson, R.D., Woolley, F.R., and Merrill, M.D. Exemplar and Non-Exemplar Variables Which Produce Correct Classification Behavior and Specified Classification Errors. *Journal of Educational Psychology,* 1972, *63,* 144-152.

SIEGFRIED ENGELMANN has engaged in teaching, research, and program development on all levels, from preschool through college. The Bereiter-Engelmann preschool was the first to demonstrate that disadvantaged preschoolers could excel in academic skills. The Engelmann-Becker Follow Through model for disadvantaged children in Kindergarten through third grade was deemed by the U.S. Office of Education to be the only effective Follow Through program. Engelmann is currently a Professor of Special Education at the University of Oregon, where he is co-director of the Direct Instruction Follow Through program. He is also a research associate at Oregon Research Institute, working on the teaching of highly unfamiliar discriminations. Engelmann is President of the Engelmann-Becker Corporation, which develops and tries out instructional material and also provides training in Direct Instruction methods. Instruction is Engelmann's primary interest. He is senior author of nine DISTAR programs (reading, arithmetic, and language); six Corrective Reading programs; two advanced arithmetic programs; programs in handwriting, creative writing, and spelling; speech, speech perception, and language programs for deaf children; instructional games; and over a dozen tests. He is author or co-author of ten books on instruction and related topics.